Through the Corridors of Black and White

AN ONGOING JOURNEY

M.L. JOSEPH

INDIA · SINGAPORE · MALAYSIA

Notion Press

No.8, 3rd Cross Street,
CIT Colony, Mylapore,
Chennai, Tamil Nadu – 600004

First Published by Notion Press 2020
Copyright © M.L. Joseph 2020
All Rights Reserved.

ISBN
Paperback 978-1-64899-656-6
Hardcase 979-8-89415-730-6

Contents

Foreword

This is my personal testimony to an Advocate who has seen the ups and downs in the legal profession with an emphasis on hard work. He says, "We have to dream big. It is during this period I realized that dreams are not automatic machines to work on their own. Dreams do not work unless and until, you work." Another interesting aspect of his book is that it is a truism that a wise person learns from the experiences of others. Indeed, ML Joseph has candidly shared his professional journey's experiences in a frank and matter of fact style in ***Through the Corridors of Black and White***. There is much to learn and to be inspired from, especially for the young entrants.

Lawyers are liars, is a common perception, but ML Joseph has very aptly emphasized - "Being honest in your approach and action will fetch you tremendous goodwill in the profession. Honesty is a prime virtue that needs to be inculcated and nurtured all through." This pearl of wisdom, if meticulously followed by every lawyer in the profession, will not only enhance the stature of the lawyer but also the entire profession, because integrity is a core human value.

Indeed, the book will be a tremendous source of inspiration for the young who are either considering Law as a profession or have entered the corridors of black and white and are challenged by its routine and procedures. ML Joseph has shared with the reader his personal experiences on establishing a successful Law Firm and has shared some intimate details for its successful operation.

This is a book I would endorse and strongly recommend to all aspirants of the legal profession to ensure that you make a success of it and bring happiness to your family. He has beautifully said and I quote "in our career journey and on most occasions, a hidden plan of our Maker reveals itself in an utmost unexpected manner and time. Patience is the key and the trust in yourself and your skills to endure the tough days alone can make you realize your full potential and purpose."

Michael Dias

Advocate, New Delhi

PRECIOUS ENDORSEMENT FROM AN INTERNAL MASTER:

Shri Ar. L. Sundaresan,

Senior Advocate, Madras High Court

President, Madras Bar Association

30.10.2020

Shri AR.L SUNDARESAN
Senior Advocate, Madras High Court,
President - The Madras Bar Association
No.101/6, Fifth Street, Padmanabha Nagar,
Adyar . Chennai – 600020.

I had the pleasure and honor of reading the draft version of my close friend's book **'Through the Corridors of Black and White'.**

The author Mr. M.L. Joseph, Advocate, has taken great pains in writing this book, of course with confidence that it will give him immense pleasure when it is completed, published and falls in the hands of readers like me.

The author deserves a pat on the back for the excellent presentation of the way he entered the profession, steadily grew in it, worked with his seniors Mr. Tomy Sebastian at Bangalore and Shri P.S. Surana Ji at Surana and Surana International Attorneys (SSIA), Chennai and confidently moved on to his own Chennai Law Associates (CLA).

He has also made reference to his parents, family members and other **'Internal Masters'**, as he calls those who have made an impact on him.

He has made the book interesting for the readers with comparisons and metaphors for all situations.

The punch lines "Rome was not built in a day" and **"a factual lawyer is an actual lawyer"** are very impressive.

Apart from placing his journey itself as an example as to how a **First Generation Lawyer** from a middle class background can survive, grow and achieve in the legal profession, he has also laid emphasis on Client management, Case management, Personal management, etc. and has come out with the Do's and Don'ts in that regard.

In a competitive field where there is room only for survival of the fittest, reading this book will help one become fitter to survive.

This book shows the utmost respect he has for his parents, seniors Mr. Tomy Sebastian and Shri P.S Surana Ji and the love and compassion he has for his colleagues, juniors and paralegal staff.

Reading this book will give tips for turning out to be a successful lawyer, team leader, an optimist and bring out the engineer from the lawyer in you.

One word - a great exercise by Mr. M.L.J.

I wish he soon writes the book on his stint with SURANAS and I write a review on that too.

God Bless.

Wish my good friend Mr MLJ all the best in all his endeavors.

ARL. SUNDARESAN
 Senior Advocate.

Glimpse of Blessings

The wishes of elders in the profession, according to me, are priceless blessings and the connection with them on day to day basis throughout the journey of practice is the most important aspect of continuous learning from them. I feel satisfied with this leg of my journey (25 years of practice and counting) from the expressions and words that have come on record from such legal luminaries in the profession. I am extremely happy to record glimpses of their blessings.

M.L. Joseph

"I recommend this book written by ML Joseph for people from both legal and non legal backgrounds as it is very educative and inspiring. My advice to the younger generation of advocates is to be totally devoted to the profession with utmost discipline and hard work in order to be a successful lawyer. My best wishes to Joseph on the occasion of completion of 25 years of practice in the legal profession."

Shri Tomy Sebastian
Senior Advocate, Karnataka High Court

"I congratulate you for writing the book. It made a very interesting reading and a learning experience. I have started utilizing many suggestions made by you in your book, for myself and for my colleagues. I thank you for the same. The chapters on management of (i) Time (ii) Clients (iii) Cases and (iv) Self, are mostly known to me and followed by me, but it is good that you have systematically put it in writing and will be very useful to our brethren at the Bar."

Shri P.S. Surana
Founder of Surana and Surana International Attorneys, Chennai

"You have remembered your gurus Mr. Tomy Sebastian and Mr. P.S. Surana and other stalwarts. I appreciate your sense of gratitude which is fully reflected.

Especially youngsters have to read your book so that they would become inspired to become good and great. Everybody is a human being but they can only be great when they start **being human**". I find great human qualities in you and your compassion for the youngsters and poor people and also your commitment towards the good cause. Please keep it up."

Justice M. Karpagavinayagam
Senior Advocate, Supreme Court of India and
Former Chief Justice of the Jharkand High Court

"Congrats. I have run through your work "Through the corridors of black and white." I am sure that young lawyers who go through the same will find it immensely useful and beneficial in moulding their career in law. More than a chronicle of your experiences in the noble profession of law it provides insights into the challenges which the system and the stakeholders have to face now. Newer challenges seem to emerge everyday and the professional has to adapt to them. This book is really a good and worthy attempt by you. Congrats again.

I wish you all the very best. May the next 25 years be more eventful, more exciting and more satisfying than the first twenty-five."

Shri R. Basant
Senior Advocate, Supreme Court of India and
Former Judge, Kerala High Court

"I would be truthful to my conscience by saying that I read this from cover to cover without skipping any passages, words or pages and would love to say there are many takeaways for me too. The most important that struck me was the statement by his first senior and uncle Mr. Tomy Sebastian that "A factual lawyer is an actual lawyer". It is true to any lawyer.

The chapters on Delegation and Time Management, Client Management, particularly A to Z of the client management are extremely useful for any individual choosing to enter this profession. Similarly, A to Z of case management is absolutely refreshing and is useful for me in my day to day practice. I am completely impressed with the way in which he expresses personality development by devoting a chapter on self-management in regard to punctuality, planning, perseverance, physical appearance, positive reputation and last but not the least, honesty. It makes a beautiful combination for a person aspiring to enter into this profession, which he ought to have.

The book has been made so easy to read not just about the journey of M.L. Joseph, but a journey of every lawyer who would like to be a "survivor" in this profession, because every "survivor" in this profession has always been "successful".

I wish M.L. Joseph continued success with the blessings of the Almighty.

My very best wishes to Joseph!!"

Shri Arvindh Pandian
(Senior Advocate, Madras High Court)

Acknowledgments

God is good and kind all the time! The hardships I underwent during my formative years turned out to carve a decent lawyer out of me. When wastages from the stone or even from gold are removed alone, a sculpture or an ornament is created. The removal act involved pain. My faith in God, my self-belief and my learning have taken me thus far in the journey through the corridors of Black and White. Thank God.

My parents deserve thanks as they are truly living Gods. My father Mr. M.T. Lonappan (an octogenarian by now) has played a vital role in shaping my career. I have dealt with it in the book at appropriate places. To make a successful career from a student with least marks in higher secondary school final, was the magic done by my father. His sacrifices and attitude of patience without asking me to contribute for the needs of the family for almost 5 years after I stepped into the profession of law, is perhaps one of the most important reasons that made the writing of this book possible. While I dedicate my career to my father, my mother also deserves praise and thanks as it was perhaps her focus on education of all her children including me, that has seen me and my other siblings settle down in 4 different careers reasonably well.

THROUGH THE CORRIDORS OF BLACK AND WHITE is my humble attempt to pay rich tributes to my '*Master*' in profession, Shri Tomy Sebastian and the '*Guru*' who taught me the nuances of a law firm, Sri P.S. Surana. The 2 mentors who shaped me over a period of 15 years deserve all the praise and thanks, as without them there would not have been much to write about my journey through the court corridors. Therefore, this book is dedicated mainly to these 2 stalwarts.

To make this publication happen, I have been pushed by my partners K. Subhashini and Amar K. Panwar at Chennai Law Associates, who have utmost respect and affection towards me. They see me at times as their friend, at times as their mentor and at times as a crisis management professional. Be that as it may, they have repeatedly insisted that I record my journey thus far in the form of a Book and that motivation was indeed the start point of writing this book. Mrs. Meera Gupta has encouraged me to refine the title of my book and contributed immensely with her time and suggestions.

My family members - my wife Minu and daughters Greetelle and Xenatelle have also played an important role in my success so far, without which this book could not have been presented in the present form.

My English master Shri P.N. Vijayan, who I am in touch with even today, is perhaps the original source of having planted the seeds of the English language within me. I owe my special thanks to my English teacher. So also, Shri R. Selvarasu, my Tamil master is yet another person responsible for some portion of success in my career of law thus far. I wholeheartedly thank him for his efforts in teaching me the classical Tamil language during my school days.

My junior and scribe Ms. Nandini Murali, BBA.LLB., dedicated her personal time while at home during the lockdown days. She also found time amidst her regular office works to assist me in writing this book. She deserves praise and thanks for the voluminous untiring effort exhibited by her in typing most of the contents, reading, aligning and making the manuscript of the book presentable for delivery to the publishers. It is she who teamed up with some dynamic young minds who entered as interns during 2018 and 2019, who mooted the idea of this book along with my partner Mrs. K. Subhashini Suresh and who participated in the finalisation of the title and suggested ideas for the format of the book. I place my appreciation and gratitude to the interns of Chennai Law Associates - Shreya Narayanan, Shridula Raj, Divya Joseph, Jino Mathews, Venkat Krishna and Amier Abbaz. The enthusiasm they exhibited was like seeds that kept growing over a period of time even in their absence.

Ms. Bindu Kundany (MS in Clinical Neuro Psychology, University of Glasgow) hailing from Olavakkode (Now Palakkad), Kerala, has been like another elder sister to me since my childhood days. She spent her quality time well past midnight on many consecutive days to carefully read and edit my manuscript and sent several audio files, recommending changes that enhanced the beauty of the book. To record her name in this page would be the smallest act of gratitude that I can do for her act of kindness.

I owe my special thanks to Mr. Alwyn Sebastian, S/o. Shri Tomy Sebastian and Mr. Verghese Vadekkathala of Bangalore, who helped me by reviewing the manuscript and giving me their quality feedback.

Before parting with acknowledgments due to all for making this book possible, I must record the pain and strain taken by one of the senior most legal professionals in the country – Mr. Michael Dias – Advocate, New Delhi, for reading the book word by word and writing its foreword. My sincere thanks is also due to Justice M. Karpagavinayagam and Justice R. Basant, both of whom have showered their blessings and affection on me and who have given their precious time to read the manuscript and acknowledge the usefulness of the book by recommending it to young readers. Senior Counsel Shri Ar. L Sundaresan and Shri Arvindh Pandian have always stood with me in my professional journey, be it the inauguration of Chennai Law Associates or the launch of Chennai Lexlight. I am very fortunate to receive their continuous support in my professional career and their recommendation for this book means a lot to me personally.

Last but not the least, professional publication carried out effectively by Notion Press deserves praise and applause.

Preface

"Enjoy the little things, for one day you may look back and realize they were the big things."

-Robert Brault, *American Operatic Tenor*

THROUGH THE CORRIDORS OF BLACK AND WHITE is my humble attempt to paint a colorful portrait of the intrinsic beauties of my journey through the court corridors thus far. This book is intended to inspire the younger generation to do well in all that they do and go for glory with their fullest energy and enthusiasm, to surge past their peers and contemporaries in their professional journey and become extremely successful in the careers of their choice.

These excerpts from my life will demonstrate patience as the key for success. 'Rome was not built in a day', goes the adage. Not all milestones in our life occur by plan. But planning your day consistently and working at it sincerely will definitely compile into a well earned successful career as days do not merely pass by and you indeed do not waste the time on hand.

Many a time a time the little things that occur on a day to day basis in our lives, be it personal or professional, did not always bring joy when such events actually took place. We had to experience pain, insult, frustration and humiliation in front of our co-workers, friends, family members or even clients at times. Little did we realize, then, the significance of such little things that shape our future in a big way at a later stage. Very rarely at a later stage of our life, do we agree and acknowledge that those little things were actually the ones which earned us big things in our lives!

Many a time, I have thought it was the end, not realizing that it was a mere bend in my path. We all consider it an accomplishment just to achieve the minimum prescribed academic qualification for any profession unaware of the fact that our anxieties and frustrations will actually settle down automatically without much of our contribution as time passes. What is destined will happen and it will happen for the good if your efforts are positive. Good begets good. I sincerely hope that this book motivates the reader in you, the young in you, the professional in you and the ever learning student in you.

'A lawyer in the making' was probably pre-written in my horoscope, though not within my knowledge, at least until I completed the higher secondary school leaving certificate course, from St. Michael's, Coimbatore in the year 1989. A coincidence which I fondly recall every now and then is a black and white photograph with a full suit in black, when I was barely 4 years old. The said photograph has to be understood in the settings of 1975 at a native village near the famous Sri Krishna Temple, Guruvayoor, which was my maternal grandparents' home. There was no camera or even a photo studio nearby. The happiness, with which my maternal aunt, Mrs. Rosy Pulikkathara, asked my father to take me in that suit to the photo studio in the nearest town about 10 Kms from my grandparents' home, is still seen in the eyes of my mother whenever she narrates this incident. It is also a pleasant coincidence that it was the same Mrs. Rosy who brought the suit material for me from the United States, for the suit I wore on my enrollment day in 1995 (20 years later). I had never worn a black suit ever since I first wore it when I was 4 right until 27.09.1995 - my enrollment day. Little did I realize that I would be wearing this attire for most of my life thereafter!

My maternal grandfather was the only person who could be related to some form or aspect of having a legal background. Even though he was an accountant for a private bank, he learnt the skill of writing documents and presenting the same for registration and he carried that profession as a document writer full time after a family owned bank where he was employed closed down due to insolvency. He was very popular and trusted and was even considered lucky by many people in and around his town and he was a busy person doing several registrations of properties and other legal documents until he passed away in 1974. It was my maternal aunt Mrs. Rosy who wrote the drafts of the documents as she had a very elegant and artistic handwriting and my grandfather also asked her to write the fair documents at times. She was so happy at the opportunity because she was given a tip, perhaps 25 *Paise* for each document that she wrote.

Apart from that, on my father's side, my grandfather was considered to be a just man who was well read and was conversant with every part of the Holy Bible and he was approached by our relatives (about 80-100 families of the Mandumpal clan, who resided within 2 Kms from my father's ancestral home) frequently for resolving property issues, family disputes, *etc.,* and I have seen him as a practical arbitrator, advising 'parties' to compromise and not even think of litigating. He had his education by getting home tuitions in those days, arranged by his father, and I am told he never received any formal schooling throughout his life. Alternate Dispute Redressal methods are being encouraged and canvassed by Courts and litigating parties are asked to explore possibilities of settlement outside court, which was virtually being done by my grandfather in those days. Even these remotest links to any form of legal activity was understood by me long after I became a lawyer- a practicing lawyer.

A career in law became the point of discussion only because of my guru (Master) Shri Tomy Sebastian, who was none other thanthe son in law of my mother's eldest sister. He was also a first generation lawyer, but was known to be amongst the top lawyers practicing on the criminal side in

Bangalore. His words and gestures kept almost everyone at bay and he was considered to be extremely short tempered and unapproachable. However, this great man liked our small house in Pothanur and the pleasant climate during summers, which brought him to our house every year. The summer of 1996 was the turning point of my life and the convincing discussions my Senior, Tomy Sebastian, had with my father resulted in me being compelled to stop all job searches abruptly and give up all positions that I was holding in the Catholic Church, which I then thought was running only because of me and which I had lot of emotional attachment towards. The decision was made within a week after Tomy Sir left our home that May and in the first week of June 1996 commenced an unimaginable journey into the Corridors of Black and White!

M.L. Joseph

The Kick Start

*"Everything you have done and been through is valuable and important.
In order to be who you are, to know what you know, to be where you are
in this moment, you needed to go through what you went through."*

-Iyanla Vanzant, *American lawyer and inspirational speaker*

I always compared my career to a scooter with electric start (and an alternate kicker for getting started), which had to be kicked often to start when batteries were out of charge, more so because the scooter was not in use for a considerable period of time.

My father was initially in private service in Chennai as an accountant for a bakery and moved on to get an employment in Signal and Telecommunication workshop of the Southern Railways, which was established in Pothanur near Coimbatore in Tamil Nadu, India. My mother was a qualified Hindi teacher, who took to full time employment in a school, only after my eldest sister was in 8th Std and I, her eldest son, was in 4th Std. She ensured that her first daughter took care of the remaining 3 of us in her absence. We all studied in the same co-education school run by the Indian Railways.

Suffice to record that there was no great lineage for me in the legal profession. This by itself was a discouraging factor for me during my law college days. My aim was to complete law and if possible, qualify myself with some additional diplomas or degrees and be gainfully employed in some company in and around Coimbatore. My internship days, which were compulsory in the final year back then, took me reluctantly to the Court corridors in Coimbatore. The Magistrate Court Complex in Coimbatore back then was a shabby building with broken windows and doors and had cobwebs in all its corners and was dusty throughout. It was commonly referred to by the public as '*Kudhiravandi Court*', which means 'horse-cart Court'. For a long time there was a stand near the Court where these horse carts used to be lined up similar to the auto rickshaw stands that we can see now. Perhaps, the Magistrate Court complex in Coimbatore got it's name from this. The combined court complex and the facilities of computer centers and Xerox copying that are available now present a whole new world for beginners in the legal profession, which was not the case back then. I went on to complete my 5 year integrated law course from the Coimbatore Law College and also did my post-graduate diploma in personnel management from the Tamil Nadu Productivity Council, Coimbatore Chapter and was running helter skelter attending interviews to somehow secure a job in a company, even while being employed as an administrative executive in a family owned electric foundry on the suburbs of Coimbatore. I was reporting to one Mr. Angaraj, an ex-lecturer of PSG College of Arts and Sciences, Coimbatore, who resigned to set up Empire Industries, the first producer of domestic washing machines in India. They were sold under the brand name 'Universal Washing Machines'.

As every young man attending interviews and expecting call letters from some companies employing them with handsome salaries and perks does, I too was getting frustrated at the lack of response and the feeling that these appointments were probably based on recommendations and thread-pulling in big organizations. Unfortunately, I had nobody to do that for me, though I would say now that I was fortunate that it turned out that way. It is not that our aspirations and expectations will be fulfilled instantly in our career journey and on most occasions, a hidden plan of our maker reveals itself in an utmost unexpected manner and time. Patience is the key and the trust in yourself and your skills to endure the tough days alone can make you realize your full potential and purpose.

Between June 1994 and June 1996, all that I did was to venture into a part time MBA Course at the Barathiyar University Campus, Coimbatore, which also I had to discontinue immediately after my first semester due to an ailing brother-in-law who required medical attention and my physical presence for a longer period and also due to lack of financial support necessary for completing the MBA.

Nothing related to the practice of law had inspired me, not even the great icon in our family, Sri Tomy Sebastian, as I did not know much about his skills or fame in the profession at that point of time, except for hearing that he was a great lawyer in Bangalore. My lack of inspiration to commence a career in litigation was due to various inexplicable reasons that kept on sending negative signals to my mind during that period of time for sure. I can say with fair certainty that the 'self start' mechanism in my scooter (career) was apparently defunct and the only way it could be started was with a tactical kick with a knack.

Within 2 weeks after Tomy Sebastian visited our house in the Summer of 1996 and spoke to my father about the possibility of me commencing practice with him, I wound up all my activities and resigned from my job with Mr. Angaraj in Coimbatore and also gave back the registers and cash book of the Catholic Youth Movement of which I was the Treasurer in my Parish Church at Pothanur, reluctantly but upon specific orders from my father as he had given his word to my guru Sri Tomy Sebastian, to send me to his Gurukul for practicing law as a profession under his able guidance. I never sensed the inbuilt incarceration that the profession of law demanded until I reached the office of Shri Tomy Sebastian. Soon I realized that the 'tactical kick'happened during May 1996 and the scooter commenced its journey thereafter from Tomy Sebastian and Associates, No. 50, III Floor, Church Street, Bangalore – 560 001."Be patient and learn what all you can from Senior and don't worry about contributing financially to our family for the next 3 to 4 years.", were the kind words uttered by a poor father in the hope of making a career in law for his son under the watchful eyes of the popular legal giant.

The Centric Catalyst

*"Change is hardest at the beginning, messiest in the middle
and best at the end."*

-Robin S. Sharma, *Indian Management Guru and Writer*

The Centric Catalyst is a chemical and its influence is silent but visible in the outcome of the medium that transformed from what it was to what it is. A lawyer par excellence, an unsurpassable orator, a strong mentor, a tough coach and a truly distinguished trial advocate beyond words, may all not be sufficient to describe the true depth of knowledge and skills that the man possesses. A truly centric catalyst was my senior ShriTomy Sebastian and I was the medium then. I use this word 'Catalyst' to describe my mentor and the priceless Senior he is till date, more so because he never changed a bit all along and his direct and indirect influences changed me from within, throughout.

Change for good or you will perish, was repeatedly hammered into my mind by the great Senior Tomy Sebastian from day 1 of my '*Gurukulvasa*' (stay in the hermit's school). Somewhere much later, I connected the efforts of my senior to a sculptor and me as the barren rock. Many wastages of the rock had to be chiseled out to shape me into the idol that is being followed, at least by a handful of juniors and staunch followers (now).

"A factual lawyer is an actual lawyer", proclaimed Shri Tomy Sebastian every now and then to all his juniors all along, highlighting the importance of mastering the facts of the cases that were being entrusted to us by him. Much later in my career, I understood the deep meaning behind his words and whenever I sat for drafting petitions, applications or even appeals, I bore this statement in mind and when I aligned the facts in sequence, I could find that the proposed reliefs could be moulded faster and more efficiently for the client and soon, I understood that when the facts were placed correctly, grievances highlighted and prayers moulded accordingly. The law, in fact, took care of itself and came to the aid of the distressed client. I consider this as the most important ingredient essential for attaining mastery in advocacy.

Any amount of praise or acknowledgment of gratitude cannot truly describe what ShriTomy Sebastian has done for me in my professional life. To term him as 'The Centric Catalyst' is what I sincerely feel can be the closest description in my words, to what he deserves from my heart. I remain fully indebted to this great Guru that he was to me throughout my tenure with him at Tomy Sebastian & Associates, Bangalore. I believe that he alone has made me what I am now. A callus on the middle finger of my right hand stand testimony to the length and volumes of dictations that were taken down from Senior in long hand with my own abbreviations with absolutely no skill of shorthand writing. The dictations that flew from my guru travelled faster than light and the vocabulary that Senior possessed were never seen by me in anyone later. The sound knowledge of English grammar that he had acquired despite having done his schooling in Malayalam medium, surprises me till this very day. A scholar of all South Indian languages and a person who mastered Hindi and Urdu to perfection, apart from his strength in English as stated above, set him a class apart.

On a lighter vein, Senior's cussing vocabulary collections in all languages known to him was also of a different league. It was so enjoyable when my foes were at the receiving end but it was unbearable when I had to receive them, seldom in private and mostly under the glare of several pairs of eyes in the office and occasionally even in courtrooms and court corridors.

Much later, I connected my guru to the character of a mechanic, which was beautifully portrayed in a Tamil Film 'Kaadhal' by none other than the award winning director Mr. Balaji Shaktivel (who in my subsequent days became a good friend of mine and also put me to the silver screen by making me a small actor donning the role of a High Court Judge in his much acclaimed award winning film 'Vazhakku en 18/9'). The mechanic in 'Kadhal' had a very peculiar way of training his assistants by flinging spanners and screwdrivers at them whenever they made a mistake in getting him the right tools while he was busy repairing the two-wheelers entrusted to him. The assistants in that mechanic shop learnt the tricks of the trade faster and became efficient mechanics much ahead of their peers working elsewhere. So did we, who flocked under the watchful eyes of the great senior Tomy Sebastian, who dedicated his precious time in dictations and advices. Time is the most precious gift that can be given to anyone by us. It cannot be purchased for money at any time later. The output of senior's sincere efforts, unmindful of the value of his time, is what has chiseled many wastages or excesses from the crude stone that I was to perhaps shape me into what I am now.

I always compared my senior colloquially to the famous jackfruit of Kerala, which is full of thorns externally and is even extremely sticky when cut open, but the edible portion of the jackfruit is extremely sweet, althoughit takes time to reach that portion of the fruit. So, don't assess people by looks and not even by the words they utter. All that matters is a kind heart and the generous personality they exhibit in their totality. Maybe the wait will differ from person to person before one can really accept the good in others. I can tell you with certainty that being patient is definitely worth its while.

Peripheral Problems

"Do not go where there is no path. Go instead where there
is no path and leave a trail."

-Ralph Waldo Emerson, American Philosopher

The tests undertaken for getting a driver's license may not be sufficient to exhibit the skills of a good driver. This fact is known to many but hard to accept. Experience in life teach us the need to keep acquiring and enhancing our skills and at times, learn absolutely new skills which will make us leave a mark and perhaps, a trail in the journey of our career undertaken by us.

My proficiency in the English language and the prizes won by me in Tamil literary competitions all through my schooling and through college were not of great advantage to me in Bangalore, as I had walked into the most busy trial advocate's office and that too an office which handled extremely critical criminal cases of grave offenders under the astute leadership of my senior and mentor.

A lawyer can only do even the least in his office only with the aid of the regional language of the territory where he practices. Bangalore therefore demanded the knowledge of Kannada as a basic qualification for a litigating lawyer to practice on the trial side of advocacy. An appellate lawyer who practices only in the High Court can manage without the knowledge of Kannada by addressing arguments in English and seeking the help of translators to understand the contents of documents which were in Kannada. Translation of Kannada documents were mandatory in the High Court as Judges got to be appointed from various parts of the country in the High Court of Karnataka as well.

I cannot forget the abusive force, although with extremely good intention, that was hurled at me by my senior to force me to learn Kannada, at least as a spoken language. Don't reflect on the words of your mentor and try to look into his genuine intentions and never forget to observe the quality time that he dedicates to guide you through the learning program during your junior days. But this is easier said than done. My colleagues would vouch that I indeed did practice it. Soon, I picked up the spoken language of Kannada and also started reading a little bit of Kannada, but I was nowhere close to Senior's expectations on that front even when I finally left for my marriage in December 2000 perhaps, for a totally different pasture altogether.

I was extensively assigned to take down dictations, which I, till date believe to be the source of legal knowledge that comes to my rescue while drafting legal documents for proceedings inside and outside courts. Even senior's tiny elephant eyes moved quickly in various angles despite his jet speed dictations. Back then, one sided cyclostyled corner stitched cause list pages (daily list of High Court cases that were circulated for a cost to all High Court advocates who subscribed to it) were being utilized for taking down dictations by juniors. Even amidst his dictation, Senior used to find my lack of noting down punctuations and words being missed by me. I could hear hushes and gushes amongst other juniors when I was with senior for a dictation session and when Senior took short breaks for recharging his imagination in isolation by standing on the steps that led to the fourth floor of our office and perhaps to prepare him for the next session of dictation. Rarely, one or two juniors would estimate his time of return and come hastily into senior's cabin to console me and feel the sadistic happiness that they enjoyed during my bad times. The rash end to the earlier session would not be recalled even slightly by the Learned Senior and the following session would start in a humorous way, asking about things which I liked and at times, by saying to me, "slightly you are better than other fools here and some English helps you to stay in my office. Okay let us start" and on goes the second session. The concluding time could never be assessed or estimated and I distinctly remember having completed some long dictations well past midnight. The time given for conversion of the said dictation to typed drafts was not more than the very next day post lunch session that would commence by 04:30 or 05:00 PM when senior would come back after a short nap from his home, if he had no pressing court work post lunch.

The rate of attrition in Tomy Sebastian Associates was very high as more often juniors could not relate to the training techniques adopted by the great senior and many wanted immediate financial returns and above all, such migratory juniors lacked patience. I did not own a two-wheeler though I had a license to drive one. I was at the mercy of my richer colleagues at office for travelling to the City Civil Court and Magistrate Court complexes initially where I was deputed by Senior. The golden idea of the other side of the river always being greener came too often to the minds of such juniors who shifted offices for flimsy reasons without understanding the value of the process of learning. Unknowingly, I started walking a path that was least travelled by and I was not sure of what was in store for me and where I was being taken to, but I could see that behind me the trail left by me by itself was making a path, perhaps for others to follow.

Money was not actually required by me in Senior's office as I stayed with my mother's eldest sister (senior's mother-in-law). I had breakfast and dinner at my aunt's house and lunch was provided to all staff, lawyers as well as paralegals, by senior from very good Andhra style restaurants in Bangalore. Senior was generous in providing office wears in dozens and multiple pairs of shoes as he was very particular that I should come well dressed to office. The occasional lunch at Hotel Raj near the City Civil Court and the delicious Chinese food from some specialized Chinese restaurants in the company of senior when we had post lunch court work is still etched in my memory. My self-recreation time was on Saturdays after office with friends and the tribe grew rapidly spending all that was earned during the week at different tables with beers, drinks and food of multiple cuisines. Little was thought on saving money then and I wandered the path of happiness and relaxation in the company of friends and colleagues and even friends of friends and friends of colleagues. It was only much later when my marriage was being arranged that I felt the pain of not having saved any money for myself. Ever since the day I took the hand of my wife Minu in marriage, I have not consumed even a drop of liquor till date. I recall distinctly that it was extremely difficult in those days to find a life partner for a young male first generation lawyer who was yet to settle down and start earning consistently. However, considering the reputation of my family and the office of Tomy Sebastian where I was a lead junior at the time, some marriage proposals were being discussed from the end of 1999 onwards. It was eventually my senior who convinced my parents to visit my wife's house back then and look at the possibilities of marrying her if all other social aspects were a match. Thus, my marriage was solemnized with Minu, D/o. Mr. KK Mathews from Thrissur, Kerala, a proposal which was initiated by ShriTomy Sebastian and his wife, Mrs. Rosy Sebastian and I am ever grateful to them for the perfect match they found for me and thus, senior had also contributed directly to the settling down of my personal life. I never asked for any monetary support from my senior for the marriage expenses, due to my personal reservations. However, the income that I was drawing and my financial situation that prevailed immediately prior to my marriage and also soon after, made me introspect whether I needed to work elsewhere outside the relationship of my strong senior and mentor and assess my strengths and weaknesses and succeed on my own with the acquired knowledge and experience. It was a tough decision to make and I had honestly let down my senior's expectations and perhaps his unrevealed plans for me. This conflict that arose within my mind and the internal debate that was going on within me, eventually made me think deeplyaboutthe future of my career in the last week of December 2000. I communicated my decision to move out of Bangalore to my senior, first over telephone. He did not relish the idea but after some ceremonial discussions over phone, I was asked to personally come and hand over all the case files to other deputed juniors and then proceed with my decision. Despite all odds and a sense of extreme insecurity, I unhesitatingly took a decision to relocate from the Las Vegas of South India to the cultural capital of India and gateway to the rest of South India – Chennai!

A New Dawn

"The life in front of you is far more important than the life behind you."

-Joel Osteen, *American pastor, televangelist, and author*

My journey to Chennai from Bangalore was more of an emotional compulsion and a strange thought of necessity for liberation from the clutches of relationships which placed me in Tomy Sebastian's office. I started feeling the necessity to move on independently after my marriage with Minu. My mother was tensed and stressed at the thought of my unemployed status just before my marriage and was not sure as to whether I had taken the correct decision in my life. Between 23rd December 2000 and 28th January 2001, I was also not sure about my future and career.

By the last week of January 2001, I had finished my handing over and relieving formalities at Tomy Sebastian and Associates and was on the lookout for a new opportunity. My wife and I are separated by 7 years and she was too young but she was very straightforward and extremely supportive during my troubled initial days when I was unemployed and uncertain of how, when and where I would settle down with my family. My father went on to the extent of suggesting that with a small income that I could generate by practicing in the District Courts at Coimbatore, I could live with my parents in the Mandumpal House at Pothanur so that I could manage my living expenses within my limited means. However, I can never forget one Mrs. Sheetal Ranjan (D/o. late Mrs. Aruna Jain, Advocate and

Feminist, Chennai), who was a good friend of mine and for whom I had successfully conducted a case at Bangalore. It was Sheetal who brought me to Chennai and introduced me to the stalwart Shri P.S. Surana, Founder and Managing Partner of Surana and Surana International Attorneys, Chennai.

The meticulous person in Shri P.S. Surana emerged on the very first day when I met him at his office on the 3rd floor of No. 224, NSC Bose Road, Chennai, exactly opposite the office of the Tamil Nadu Bar Council, when he took down, in his own handwriting, notes of my interview while he was conducting it. The path making interview lasted for almost 90 minutes and by the end of it, Surana Sir asked me about my 'expectation' and there was mutual agreement on it immediately. He wanted me to join at the earliest and on 09.02.2001, I joined the office of Shri P.S. SuranaJi, which was one of the most prized moments of my career in law. I am at a loss for words to describe the love and affection that Shri P.S. SuranaJi showered on me throughout my long tenure of almost a decade with him and his highly reputed law firm. At work, Surana Sir was a strict and meticulous boss and was highly demanding. The long time he spent on discussions with me on specific cases that he chose to entrust me and the stage wise positive outcome that he would sit and assess personally with me, are all inscribed in golden letters in my mind even now. The affection he showed on my wife, more so as a daughter, apparently, since he had none, and the care he showed in her studies by periodically following up where she stood in her course are precious investments that were made by him for the welfare of my family, also by enhancing my salary from time to time to ensure that I did not depend on anyone for my financial requirements.It was with his direct involvement that my wife's bachelor's degree in physiotherapy, which she was pursuing in a private college in Chennai from July 2001 onwards, became a reality. These are unparalleled acts of the most respected person in my life, Shri P.S. SuranaJi. I will fail miserably if I do not record the apt and perhaps, a kinder approach taken by Smt. Leela Surana Ji on all these fronts and I never felt that I was living away from my parents at any point of time when I was at Surana and Surana.

The very first case that was entrusted to me by Surana Sir was a case for money recovery to the tune of almost Rs. 100,00,00,000/- (Rupees One Hundred Crores). Cases were filed in the year 2000 against the State of Kerala owned Keltron. The immediate challenge was to draft a legal notice that spelt the proposed legal action on the civil suit for money recovery, company winding petition as well as writ petition against the State of Kerala. There was a Governor's guarantee involved as a document in the said file, securing the repayment to the Calcutta based financial institution that lent money to the State owned Keltron. Subsequent to the successful drafting and issuance of the legal notice after finalization by Surana Sir, I was entrusted the cases to be filed in the High Court of Kerala at Ernakulam. I filed a company petition seeking the relief of winding up the company Keltron as it failed to pay its admitted dues. On the basis of the Governor's guarantee, a Writ was also filed. After the issuance of notice on admission, Keltron engaged one of the senior most Senior Advocates in Kerala, Mr. Kelu Nambiar (now no more). The anxiety with which I reported the developments with regard to the engagement of a senior counsel by the opposite party was received surprisingly without any reaction and with extreme calmness by Surana Sir. The faith he imposed on me brought tears to my eyes instantly. "You will do this case come what may, as against that very senior. You know the facts better than anyone else and I am sure you will succeed. In this case, I will not approve of engaging any senior", were the kind words he told me that inspired me to take up the challenge, although I was a little David in front of the Goliath – Adv. Shri Kelu Nambiar. The case went on for almost a year and the entire money was recovered in the process, thanks to a wonderful order from His Lordship Mr. Justice Thottathil Radhakrishnan, who recorded the admissions of Keltron and the said order brought about a settlement between the disputing parties and the case was being called on a monthly basis for reporting receipts of installments by the finance company as from the State of Kerala as per the recorded agreement. I also have to necessarily add the affection that was showered on me by Advocate Shri Kelu Nambiar, who went on to become very close to me in the latter years and I had met with him more than twice after the case got over just to seek his blessings, which he was very happy to oblige. It was only much laterthatI heard about the sad demise of the Senior Advocate Shri Kelu Nambiar in September 2012. The Keltron case was just the beginning of my long and successful tenure at Surana and Surana – a law firm of international repute.

I went on to bring glory to Surana and Surana and was directly reporting to Shri P.S. SuranaJi, who by the beginning of 2001 itself, commenced his spiritual journey deep into one of the most scientific and prolific religions of our country 'Jainism'. Soon, I could connect with the powerful Jain Navkar Mantra which goes as follows:

Ṇamōarihantāṇaṁ

Ṇamōsiddhāṇaṁ

Ṇamōāyariyāṇaṁ

Ṇamōuvajjhāyāṇaṁ

Ṇamōlōēsavvasāhūṇaṁ

The meaning of the above Mantra is as follows:

I bow to the (arihants) liberated ones

I bow to the (siddhas) perfected ones

I bow to the (acharyas) preceptors

I bow to the (Upadhyâyas) teachers

I bow to all the (sadhus) saints

To be humble and to pay respect to all the above category of people such as the liberated souls, masters (persons who achieve perfection), spiritual gurus (persons capable of training the teachers), teachers themselves and saints (humans who achieve god's prized and intimate position) was perhaps being reiterated by chanting the above mantra/stotra as I could understand closely from observation and interaction with Shri P.S. SuranaJi. How can I forget the "CHATURMAS PRAVESH" for which I had joined Shri Surana Ji from the outskirts of Bangalore almost at Kengeri on the Mysore Road after walking with the Jain Acharyas who were commencing their 'CHATUR MASYA', the 4 months which they spend in meditation, prayers and spiritual sermons and undertaking fasts every year. These Jain *Acharyas* never travel by any method of transport apart from their own legs, throughout their life. For 8 months in a year, they travel bare foot from village to village, town to town, and stay anywhere between 1 day and 29 days depending on several factors, preach spirituality, morals and ethics and persuade the public to lead a virtuous life. In the rainy season consisting of 4 months in a year, they do not travel, lest while travelling even on foot they may trample on insects etc. which abound in rainy season. Therefore, during those 4 months, they stay at one place, keeping their outside physical movements to the barest minimum and concentrate on meditation, prayers and spiritual sermons..

Whenever criticism arose, SuranaJi wanted to prove himself through his work and not by his words. I would say he was the most influential personality in my career who inculcated professionalism in me and in all what I do. A true leader should lead by example and look into each and every requirement of his followers, materialistic requirements as well as spiritual and personal requirements too and keep a check on any aspect that could distract and derail the focus of his followers individually. A hard task seldom followed by many leaders, was practiced to perfection by Shri P.S. SuranaJi. His sense of humor and the knack of uncomplicating the complicated stuff when it comes to work, segregating it chronologically and segmenting it for easier tackle, made voluminous work look easy and move faster than anticipated..

Surana and Surana was rated as the best law firm for the entire of South India and boasted of a strong team on all practice areas of law and was indeed a 'full service law firm'. The ISO certification for the law firm, perhaps the only one then in Chennai, was definitely a worthy achievement for the system management in a law firm. Here, I saw documentation for the day's work when it began and when it ended and the follow up activities were also generated systematically to the juniors/paralegals who were deputed for the respective cases. Thus, in all, there was a system of supervision and corrective measures, if rarely something went wrong, which I had not seen in my previous office. It is at Surana's that I could understand that law was being practiced in two streams, namely, lawyers who practiced law in the areas of their specialization and as a practice, lawyers who established firms and practiced all areas of law by engaging specialists in the respective fields and thereby carrying on the practice of law in a different manner. The required infrastructure for the former was very little and the practice was centered on the all important senior of that office. Whereas, the infrastructure for the latter had to be of the expected corporate standards and an established hierarchy of management to administer the human resources and specific teams to manage the commercial aspects that arose in the day to day business, apart from achieving focused success on all matters that were entrusted by the clients, had to be put in place. The practice areas never exclusively centered on senior professionals in the said firm as there were practice areas that were being outsourced to expert professionals sitting outside the firm's premises as well. I must admit that until then, perhaps I was a horse capable of taking to the tracks of the racecourse, but with blinkers on to have a focused approach devoid of distractions in my earlier stream of practice under the astute leadership of Mr. Tomy Sebastian, the much acclaimed criminal lawyer of Bangalore city.

I started seeing a whole new world with awe and definitely, the dawn of 9th February 2001 was a new dawn in all aspects for me and my wife Minu.

The Stage

"All the world's a stage,
And all the men and women merely players;
They have their exits and their entrances;
And one man in his time plays many parts;"

-William Shakespeare

Very soon after I joined the firm, SuranaJi found me to be capable of playing many roles. My entry into the firm was to assist a retired Magistrate Shri Muni Rao, who was the one man army, practicing criminal law in the firm. My exposure to other areas of practice commenced in no time and the drafting skills sown in me and honed by my guru for the past 5 years came to my rescue and the legal notices and multi-pronged attacks in the initial notices and exchange of replies in response to legal notices received by the firm's clients that were being drafted by me caught the attention of SuranaJi. In about six months' time, i.e., by 15th August 2001, my first birthday celebrated at Surana and Surana, I was quite popular amongst my colleagues and I was introduced to every person who visited the firm, specially by SuranaJi. I was given additional responsibilities of attending to hand-picked civil cases and to conduct all the criminal cases at all stages by then. By the end of 2001, Shri Muni Rao fell ill and some new teammates were inducted and there was a full fledged criminal law division by then, under my leadership.

The Criminal Law Division was a part of the litigation team and I remember a Cheque dishonor case, where the client happened to be M/s. Colgate Palmolive Ltd., and the accused was a person by name Manjula and the statutory notice under S. 138 of the Negotiable Instruments Act was issued by the company. The statutory notice contained the demand for repayment of amounts covered by 16 dishonored cheques. The divergent opinions of 2 Single Judges of the Madras High Court led to the initiation of a reference by the 3rd Judge and thereafter, the matter was placed before a Division Bench and a case came to be reported in 2006 (5) CTC 303 and in 2007 (1) MLJ (Crl) 140, holding that multiple dishonored cheques can be subjected to a single statutory notice and all the causes of action merged into one cause of action and therefore, the complaint was not vitiated in law on that aspect. It is a matter of pride for me that the decision was rendered by Hon'ble Mr. Justice Sathasivam, who went on to become the Chief Justice of India and Governor of Kerala and the companion Judge was none other than Hon'ble Mr. Justice S. Manikumar, who is now the Chief Justice of Kerala High Court and the Respondent's counsel Mr. Kannan (as he then was) went on to become Hon'ble Mr. Justice Kannan of the Punjab and Haryana High Court. The point of law that was discussed and the resultant judgment was the first of its kind from the Madras High Court and which decision was referred to several times in the past, the latest being in a case reported in 2019 (4) Crimes 82 from the Karnataka High Court. To work with such people of eminence in the legal field would not have been possible if the stage was not set for me by SuranaJi. The client was a prestigious corporate and the matter was legally special and important for an entire branch of statutory practice (practitioners who specialize in cheque bounce cases), and yet the trust imposed on me by Surana Sir was way beyond my expectation back in 2002 itself not only when the original petition was filed to quash the complaint against Manjula but till the final verdict was pronounced by the Division Bench on 12.10.2006. Normally, in such cases senior counsel engagement was the order of the day but Surana Sir kept on telling me that I must do it all by myself.

Many cases followed and amongst the notable ones, is a case reported in 2005 (1) MadWN (Cri) 118 which was a quash petition that was drafted, filed and argued all by myself in respect of a senior central government officer who was falsely implicated in a corruption case and after the quash was allowed, the same was challenged in the Supreme Court by CBI. The Supreme Court had set aside the quash order and remanded the case back for trial and in the trial which I conducted. The said lady officer was acquitted of all charges on the penultimate day of her retirement. The joy and gratitude she expressed by hugging me in the Court corridors after finding out which court hall I was available in after the judgment was pronounced, are etched green in my memory till date. The job satisfaction that I derived from such orders was indeed unexplainable. The sense of achievement of success when the beneficiary (client) expresses gratitude in person, emotionally at times, are in fact the real rewards of hard work that can never be taken away from you by anyone. Nevertheless, a big stage and a wide audience and special and complicated matters being handed over to you should not be viewed as work load and should rather be treated as challenges to be overcome. When you overcome such challenges, you become worthy of the trust imposed on you, not only by the employer but also by the client. Visibility of a lawyer in Courts and the matters that he argues are very important to project a lawyer as a valuable asset. In terms of these ingredients, no stage better than the law firm 'Surana and Surana International Attorneys' could have given me the right exposure at my entry stage into the firm itself.

A partition suit between a brother and his sister was pending for 4 decades in the High Court of Madras when I was entrusted to appear. The final decree proceeding arising out of the said partition suit resulted in a mediation talk held by the Learned Judge in his chamber and the subsequent 3 sessions in the chambers of His Lordship Mr. Justice V. Ramasubramanian, (as he then was in-charge of the said portfolio in Madras High Court) saw the end of the litigation between the brother and sister. The property got released for a bigger joint venture, which benefitted the brother in a big way and in the end, it was a win-win situation for all and the 40 year old case came to an end. Alternate Dispute Redressal (ADR) methods were nascent at that time, but the zeal and interest shown by the Learned Judge opened a new learning of settling disputes out of court and that too, in matters of emotional entanglement, which was very much visible in this case.

Similarly in another case of a company winding up petition initiated by a brother's family against another brother, both of whom were into construction business, came up before Hon'ble Mrs. Justice ChitraVenkatraman in the year 2007 and my opponent counsel was a well established senior, but once again Surana sir imposed extreme confidence on me and insisted that I do the matter without engaging any senior counsel. The experience I gained in the earlier partition settlement was put to use reasonably well by me and the whole matter came to be settled after mediation was taken up at the Mediation Centre of the Madras High Court, but more so due to the tactful tagging of the civil suit and the company petition and bringing them before the very same Judge, Hon'ble Mrs. ChitraVenkatraman. Amicable sharing of ancestral properties and payment of the differential amount to one of the brothers was the end result and the happiness in all the brothers pursuant to the closure of the cases cannot be explained in words. The respect for lawyers can only increase if such win-win situations are attempted and achieved repeatedly as much as possible rather than sticking on to prove a point and getting it adjudicated and winning the case. I learnt that **winning the cause is much bigger than winning a case.**

The parents of a husband from Ooty were implicated in a case of Dowry death and the trial court had given 7 years imprisonment and sent them to custody after pronouncing the judgment, which I distinctly remember, was on a Thursday. The judgment copy and connected papers reached our office on the next afternoon, i.e., on Friday. The abetment of suicide was negated by the trial court and cruelty charges were held to be proved. Perhaps the learned trial Judge went on to convict the accused husband for dowry death, merely looking at the years of marriage (death within 7 years of marriage is the criteria under Section 304B IPC) without reframing or modifying the charges. The appeal and interim application for suspension of sentence were made ready on the Saturday and Sunday that followed. The criminal appeal was filed on Monday and moved on Tuesday before His Lordship Hon'ble Mr. Justice V. Kanakaraj. The case was that abetment of suicide and cruelty charges were made and the conviction was given for dowry death punishable under Section 304B of the IPC, without framing or modifying the charge. The law, as it stood then, did not permit such conviction and the High Court intervened and quashed that portion of the conviction at the admission stage itself. Thereby, the parents of the husband were granted relief of the suspension of sentence then and there at the admission stage itself.

Another special case that deserves a mention is a contested family case that I conducted on behalf of the husband who was 62 years old at the time, as against his wife who was 64. The husband went on to become my friend and recently passed away due to a chronic ischemic lung disease. A case for divorce was filed by the wife and being contested by the husband. In parallel, the wife initiated a bigamy case against the husband and his paramour, since a child was born to the said paramour. The bigamy case was a technical case as begetting a child from another woman other than the wife was not an offence, though it was immoral. The offence in the book was marrying again during the lifetime of the spouse without their marriage being dissolved. The date and place of the alleged second marriage and the witnesses to it were, according to the husband, imaginary and he insisted that he had not married the said paramour though he admitted that he had begotten a son from her. The facts were so nasty to the ears but the case had to be nevertheless, handled carefully. My interactions with the wife (complainant) outside the Magistrate Court at Egmore and the cross examination done to her and her witnesses and the documentary evidences that we could produce during the trial of the case to show that neither the husband nor the paramour nor the principal eye witness to the alleged second marriage could have been present on the alleged date of the said marriage at the place mentioned in the complaint, initiated a settlement. The contested divorce petition and the bigamy complaint were withdrawn by the wife and a consent petition for divorce was filed mutually. The proceedings between the parties had gone on for more than 6 years with several visits to the High Court with revision petitions filed either by the husband or by the wife at different points of time.

Arguing cases and applications in Rent Control Courts, City Civil Courts, Family Courts, Debt Recovery Tribunal (and appellate tribunal), Trademark Registry, Intellectual Property Appellate Board, Railway Tribunal, Magistrate Courts and Sessions Courts, apart from the High Courts of Madras, Karnataka, Kerala, Delhi, Punjab and Haryana, Andhra Pradesh and Mumbai kept me busy all the time and the countless number of advocate friends at all levels in all these courts earned me a face value during the decade long stay at Surana and Surana. I cherish all those memories and opportunities and by the name of a client I can even now recall the extent of work and the orders that were obtained from different Courts for that client. I am not sure how many of the young lawyers will get such a perfect stage to launch their talents. I have one thing to say though, shifting offices due to minor dissatisfactions at work and changing your mentor very often does no good for the future of your career. Very rarely can one succeed if they attempt at migration all the time.

Throughout my journey at Surana, I always kept remembering that 'the world is a stage and we, actors'. Age was catching up with me and I always wanted to open my own law firm, more so after my impressive stint at Surana's. The thought of encashing my talents for myself started coming into me by the end of 2009 and this desire pushed me hard to express it to SuranaJi freely and frankly and the Christmas season of 2009 was the best and perhaps destined time for this to happen. The grand stage, i.e., Surana and Surana International Attorneys was about to become a scene of the past as the curtains were being lifted, clearing the view, perhaps for a totally different role and a brand new scene which was unfurling. Even the good of everything must end one day until the best of something is achieved. After my initial two years at Surana and Surana International Attorneys, I found myself at the helm of affairs of the entire litigation team. Soon I was made deputy to the ever smiling and extremely hardworking Partner of Surana & Surana - Shri Kalyan Jhabak. We had a wonderful team of young and dynamic lawyers there at SSIA. Rajnikant Madhavan followed Sudhir Raja Ravindran as IP-Head. Two outstanding persons Surya Senthil and Lakshmi Devi joined the IP team and later on Rajinikanth left. Rajini and Surya Senthil were my neighbors at Trustpuram, Kodambakkam, where I live even now. Many intellectual juniors were appointed at SSIA and the vision of Surana sir to tap the young talents was indeed yielding very good results. There was also a lot of attrition at SSIA due to many factors. Young lawyers from different parts of the country being appointed straight from various good law schools was however the prime reason. They wanted to get back to their places and families after some time. I stood foot there and went on to accumulate knowledge and also grew day after day. It soon happened that my name got merged with Surana and I was being called by some high court Judges fondly as 'Joseph Surana'.

The use of technology for enhancement of one's work efficiency was the main thrust at SSIA. The access to web libraries and separate email ids for each person employed at Surana was quite astonishing back in 2000 and 2001. The use of Intranet to communicate internal circulars and use of one side papers for drafting purposes were some measures taken in the interest of the environment. The quality consciousness nurtured by the top management was visible in getting ISO certification and the Social Accountability certification and in conducting audits religiously for proper upkeep of the certificates so obtained. The necessity to maintain records as mandatory compliance to ISO requirements penetrated even to the last in the office hierarchy-the office assistants and Xerox staff etc., High quality servers and back up facilities to preserve data and its confidentiality were taken care of seriously by the management. Lunch was provided free for all at SSIA and from a top class vegetarian restaurant. Great care for Human resources was taken by the Family owned management at SSIA.

I was asked to lead the litigation team of Surana and Surana in all courts including the High court apart from travelling to other High courts in the country. I survived with ease and carried the burden with little fuss and I can say honestly that it was this period that made me visible in the High court and all the trial courts in and around Chennai. I simply loved all the attention I was getting in the firm as well as outside. Variety of works which I did during my younger days gives me an edge over my competitors even now. Never treat a work as less significant that which is entrusted to you and don't ever compare the work given to your colleagues with the work given to you. It will not only distract you but also block your mind from creatively doing the work on hand to the best of your abilities. Never push what you can do today to tomorrow. Pendency of work with you for a longer time will restrict further work allotment to you. I learnt these priceless lessons at SSIA.

Soon, opportunities rushed to me from the Police academy, delegation of German judges, Tamil Nadu Judicial Academy, Chambers of Commerce and various other institutions to present Guest Lectures as a representative of Surana and Surana International Attorneys. I grabbed it with both hands and made my presence felt and stamped my signature in those sessions as well. Do not avoid any work that is assigned to you by the leader. Do it with your inputs and style. Leave an imprint of your signature in all that you do, big or small.

I must admit that my launch into the judicial space by the master Shri P.S.S sir was perfect and all I had to do was keep functioning with all my abilities and talents as much as I can, which I honestly believe to have performed throughout my tenure there.

The Michigan case and a few other memorable cases:

I My first trip to a foreign country was to the United States of America – thanks to Shri. P.S. SuranaJi. I still remember the question of the interviewer at the US Embassy at Chennai. Are there no lawyers in U.S? I answered, it is the desire of a convict's parents that I facilitate a post-conviction appeal after discussion with an attorney and the convict. My Visa was granted for a single entry then.

I worked on proper exchange of emails to the Macombe Correctional facility (jail), where the convict was undergoing the sentence of life imprisonment and had my appointments scheduled even prior to getting my VISA. There, life Imprisonment means imprisonment throughout his life. There was no premature commutation or earlier release possible. I met Mr. Stuart Friedman at Detroit and worked with him on a motion for remand of the case for a De-Novo Trial. The only ground was ineffectiveness of the defense counsel during trial. The said defense attorney was appointed by the state to provide free legal aid as part of consular assistance to the foreign under-trial prisoner that the convict was back then. During the trip I visited New York and also interacted with another counsel Mr. Douglas Rosenthal, in respect of an earlier case for recovery of money in the Civil Courts at New York. I was quite astonished to see the lawyers working in New York and Detroit and also the function of courts in the US back then. E-filing was already in practice prior to the year 2003 itself. Court fee was being transferred to the Court registrars account by fund transfer from the authorized attorney's bank account.

The convict in Michigan was a young Indian Engineer who was too good with computers. His parents were residing in Karnataka,

India. The trial was adjudged by a Jury. The allegation was that of Manslaughter of his fiance's sister's husband who happened to be a doctor. An unwinding session during a weekend ended up in the doctor calling the mother of the accused a prostitute. The enraged son pushed the doctor to the floor and attempted to strangulate the doctor with the cable of the keyboard of a computer as the doctor lay on the floor. The accused then reached for a knife that was on the table and slit the throat of the doctor. This was the case of the prosecution. Thereafter, he picked up some jewelry and discarded them at different places alongwith the knife etc., while escaping from the scene, to make it appear that the crime was a murder for gain. The wife of the Doctor was away in another American State due to her work. The convict however stated that his knees bent unexpectedly as he was teasing the doctor after the wordy quarrel when the doctor was lying on the floor and said that the knife pierced the neck accidently. The defense counsel failed to sell this theory and did not effectively defend the accused during trial. Therefore the trial ended in conviction and life imprisonment for the convict was the sentence awarded. While reading the records of the case I noticed that the entire trial was being audio-taped by the court and then given to authorized professionals for transcription. The Trial transcripts are the depositions in the case. A fixed number of lines were allotted per page and the transcripts were being converted as it is into the format to for part of trial record. I also remember clearly about the polygraph test which the accused was asked undergo by the Inspector. He failed, leading him to a confession. The safeguards to be adopted by the magistrate while recording a section 164 statement in the nature of a confession or an admission to the crime, is also mandated in American Law. However the power vests with the Investigating officer and the warnings are called Miranda warnings. Miranda warnings came as guidelines from the Apex court of America in State v Miranda.

Consular access was provided and the accused had spoken to his attorney even before the polygraph test was undertaken by him was the case of the prosecution. Convict stated that he was rushed into the polygraph and confession without waiting for his counsel to come personally. The trial for criminal offence in the State of Michigan was by Jury method. The responsibility of the Police ended once a charge was framed by the Jury. Thereafter the entire onus or burden of proof was on the accused to prove his innocence beyond reasonable doubt. In the present case the accused could not afford a defense attorney as he was not financially capable. The state provided legal aid and a defense attorney was appointed to take up the case. As stated above, after the trial was over, there was accusation on the said defense attorney with regard to his inefficiency. The motion for remand was unsuccessful and the convict remains confined to the correctional facility. This experience facilitated immense learning in me individually and opened up new perspectives in me. It was only eight years later, in 2011, that I visited the United States of America again, this time with my parents and this time the U.S. Embassy granted me a multiple entries Visa for 10 Years.

II Yet another memorable case was that of elderly couple who were contesting for Divorce. The husband was aged 62 and was younger to his wife by 3 years. The wife was a British national who married the man after converting herself to Hinduism before the AryaSamaj at Mumbai. Her man got her Divorce from her previous husband –an Anglo Indian. Her father was on good terms with her husband even as the couple was fighting in the family court and criminal courts. Both parties alleged infidelity on each other. After a long drawn litigation, better senses prevailed on them and an out of court settlement that was mooted for by me worked wonders due to the cooperation extended by the counsel for the wife, a father son duo—Mr. N.D. Bahetty and Siddharth Bahetty. A proper settlement was recorded and divorce was granted after payment of permanent alimony to the wife and a bigamy complaint pending in the criminal court was also withdrawn. The said case provided immense procedural learning for me in the family courtand it was in accordance with trial procedure in a warrant case instituted otherwise than upon a Police Complaint.

III   A child was diagnosed of appendicitis. She was under the care of a leading pediatric surgeon in the City. He instructed immediate admission. Next day morning blood samples were drawn and sent to Lister laboratory to check for Dengue fever. Before the lab report came, the child was operated upon. Tragically, she died the very next day due to internal hemorrhage. A case for medical negligence was filed and prosecuted till the last and compensation was ordered to the parents of the child by the Hon'ble Tamil Nadu Consumer Disputes Redressal Commission.

IV   In a case before the Railway Tribunal Chennai, the huge cost of more than Rs.1 Crore was retained by the Railways for transportation of rice bags from Tuticorin to New Delhi, stating that the rice bags were stolen property from the Civil Supplies Department and that they were seized even before loading and that therefore, despite the train not moving from Tuticorin, the Railways Department was not liable to refund the money. Interpreting the Indian Contract Act and the transporter being a bonafide person who was not connected to the crime and also in view of the Freight Rules regarding booking and cancellation of Indian Railways, the Railway Tribunal ordered full refund to the Petitioner. The case was won for the client.

Dedicate fully to each and every case that is given to you. Get attached to the cause in the case. Burn the midnight oil and see what you can do for the client with all your ability. Keep doing your best at all stages of the case. Get the confidence of the client to the fullest possible extent. Ensure that he has got belief that you can sail him through the present crisis but at the same time, don't give false promises. It is equally important not to keep pressing the panic button so as to threaten the client of an adverse result in his case.

I should, in fact, put more time and write a separate book on my life at 'Suranas' as this book 'Through the corridors of black and white' will have to address many other aspects of the legal journey I have travelled thus far.

Transition

"When life throws lemons at you, pick them up and make yourself some cool lemonade."

My wife and I decided we were ready to move into the next phase of our married life. In April 2003, Minu suffered a miscarriage. She was also slightly concerned about her studies as she was pursuing a Bachelor's Degree in Pysiotherapy in private College affiliated to Dr. MGR Medical University in Chennai. I assured her that I will stand with her to complete her studies at any cost and that this need not bother her.

By the beginning of 2004, I was an expecting father and our daughter Greetelle was born on 10th September 2004 in Thrissur, Kerala. My wife was still pursuing her studies in the Physiotherapy College. She went on maternity leave and rejoined the course in June 2005. My daughter and wife joined me by the end of March 2005. Greetelle was 6 months old by then. The baby sitter, who took care of my wife when she was an infant, came with us to take care of Greetelle and she was with us until Greetelle turned 14. Minu had left to stay with her parents at Kerala in June 2004. Between June 2004 and March 2005, I was provided lunch and dinner by Mrs. LeelaSurana. The only condition was that I should have my dinner with Senior PSS before sunset as was his practice, which is a scientific Jain practice. I am ever indebted to them for the love and affection they showered on me.

By June 2005, Surana sir was asking me not take my child and Minu on bike anymore. I was also looking to purchase a car. Owning a car was becoming a necessity after Greetelle was born. Even now Minu and myself love the bike rides much more that our journeys in car. It was also an emotive compulsion for me to satisfy my mother back home. With news of each of my cousins purchasing different brands of cars year after year, there was a sense of disappointment on my mother's face more due to the fact that I didn't own a car back then. I wanted to buy a Diesel Car with a boot and therefore I needed to buy a diesel Sedan and my natural choice was Tata Indigo and it was well within my budget too. By the end of July 2005 and much before Greetelle's first birthday, I was having a car – the Tata Indigo-LX. The monthly installment amount I had to pay for it was enhanced generously by the management of SSIA. I learnt how to drive a car only after I purchased one. I then obtained my driver's license. The joy of our first car and the happiness of my aged parents when they travelled with Greetelle in the limelight to Holy Shrine of Mother Mary at Velankanni (a pilgrim Centre in Tamil Nadu) is not describable in words. I experienced that happiness joyfully throughout those days. I went on to purchase three different and bigger cars thereafter. But I have no hesitation to record here that the change of class was only due to the kind act of Shri. P.S. Suranaji. As a leader he always wanted his people to have the best lifestyle and all the comforts for their families. There are many incidents that make my eyes moist even now when I recall my life during those days.

In 2006 August (24-08-2006) my second daughter was born. She was named Xenatelle. At this juncture there were almost strict orders from the university that Minu's admission will be cancelled and that further leave cannot be granted. After a semi legal battle with the University and after paying a fine, her absence was condoned and she was granted readmission to her course after Xenatelle was born. Minu completed her 4 ½ year course in 7 years time. But the difference was that she not only had a Bachelor degree in Physiotherapy but also two lovely daughters during the said period. Greetelle and Xenatelle change our world upside down. They kept us busy. When Xena was born we had a car already and we were in the next class of the society, courtesy P.S.S. sir. The credit goes entirely to him. Both my daughters were put into a conservative traditional convent school, in Nungambakkam Chennai which is hardly 2 Kms from our house. The kindergarten days of my two daughters and their school activities brought immense joy to us. They are growing up in a wholesome manner- the sole purpose for which is that they were put into such a school. The lifestyle enhancement and transformation that occurred for me is entirely owed to the great soul, Shri PS SuranaJi.

We have to dream big. It is during this period I realized that dreams are not automatic machines to work on their own. Dreams do not work unless and until you work.

19th February 2009 saw a bizarre incident when there was a violent clash between lawyers in the High Court Premises. It was a riot involving stone-pelting by lawyers and lathi charge by police everywhere. There is no need to recall the horror. I was arguing a case in a court hall in the Annexed Building of the High Court. My Junior Amar Panwar was there. My car was parked inside the Court parking space which was seeing the riot in its fullest. So I decided to bring it out and park it on the roadside opposite to my office so that I could keep an eye on the car. Within five minutes of me parking the car I saw a group of uniformed police known as Rapid Action Force marching across and looking for advocate stickers on car windshields and breaking them. Helplessly, I saw my car windshield being broken in front of my eyes, though from the first floor of my office. Later I found that my car door lock was damaged and the back windshield broken. Next day I dropped the car for service and presented my insurance claim for the same. As I walked into TATA service Centre, I saw an advertisement for exchange of old car. I worked on that offer and moved into the next segment of car and soon I owned a brand new TATA Safari, an SUV. This time I had organized my funds and kept it a secret and was coming to office on a scooter for the next 45 days. When my new car was delivered, my complete family and I took it to Surana Sir and sentimentally took the new car key from none other than Shri. P.S. Suranaji. I saw the happiness in his eyes. He wished us good luck and gladly obliged to do the honor, by handing over the car keys officially as requested by Minu and me. My happiness was at its peak. I always wanted to own a Tata Safari from my junior days at Bangalore. Back then I was attending, in Pondicherry, a cheque bounce case of a rich friend of my Senior Tomy sir. That rich client owned a Tata Safari and we used to travel between Bangalore and Pondicherry by that luxury car in 1998-99. I used to tell myself that I will own this very car one day. My dream came true 10 years later.

Never take any mishap as a negative incident. Look at the opportunity it presents. Think well and take bold decisions. Only then you can enjoy the world even during the so called dark days. Come out of the bad moments as fast as possible and work towards making the situation brighter and bigger than it really was even before. Transition of lifestyles and moving from one segment of the society to another is never going to happen without your effort and consistent approach towards it. I must say that each and everything in my house at Chennai belongs to me and Minu and they have been collected with our efforts. Neither of us has taken any help from our parents for our household at any point of time. To live a big life and give an even bigger life to the promised ones-your spouse and family, was always in me and I must say that I moved through the transition phase with the help of God and the Godly man Shri P.S. Surana Ji.

Miracle Of Birth

"And suddenly you know: it's time to start something new and trust the magic of new beginnings"

-Meister Eckhart, German theologian, philosopher and mystic.

The labour that went into the making of CHENNAI LAW ASSOCIATES cannot be restricted to a mere 27 days - the days between my resignation at Surana (23.12.2009) and the birth of Chennai Law Associates (20.01.2010). I conceived the idea of setting up a law firm on my birthday in August 2009 and the turmoil that went into me for choosing the time to spell it out to my then boss was weighing on me heavily during those days. 'Who will join me?', 'Who will give me cases?', 'What will SuranaJi think of me?', 'At age 38, is it not too late to start all over?', 'What will happen to my financial needs and security?', etc., were only some of the questions that were popping through to the display screen of my mobile – mind -, delaying the communication of my decision to Surana Sir. The said period was indeed laborious and painful and perhaps, I experienced the pain of conceiving and holding on to a concept in mind and waiting for the delivery date as is experienced by any pregnant woman. Come what may, I will tell this before this year ends and 2010 will definitely see the beginning of my new conceptual law firm, I decided.

There was no financial difficulty to meet my family requirements anymore. Minu had completed her studies and was interning with a group of intellectuals – US return physical therapists at T-Nagar, Chennai. Both my daughters were in school and I was on the verge of turning 40. From August 2009, the thought of doing something on my own started visiting my mind intermittently. I was afraid of getting stuck as an employee of the Law Firm forever. I wanted to do something BIG. Am I destined to be this way for the rest of my life?

At times I also felt it is easier to criticize than to get the job done with the available resources in a given time. Often litigation is like a game of CHESS. All the mistakes made by the players are visible in a magnified manner to all the viewers watching from outside. At the same time it is also a team game like football. No goal can be scored if the players choose to play all by themselves and decide not to pass the ball to a more appropriate player who had less defenders near him and who could score a goal more easily.

Why shouldn't I have my own practice? What should be the model? Should it be a conservative practice of an individual lawyer or should it be a small law firm which provides quality services at affordable cost? These questions kept ringing in my head repeatedly for the next few months.

I realized that the vehicle (MLJ as I was addressed in SSIA) needed a 'Complete Overhaul'. Even though the spares were being replaced and the vehicle was being upgraded from time to time, I started feeling that the drive has been going on for too long although the distance covered had been phenomenal. A strange feeling of fatigue started creeping inside me. The journeys undertaken by me to different courts including the High Courts of Kerala, Karnataka, Andhra Pradesh, Delhi, Punjab & Haryana and Mumbai till then and the interactions I had with many senior counsels and advocates through the length and breadth of our country during my tenure and the rich experience of almost fifteen years by then started prompting from within, "Start now-on your own" and "Either now or Never". These inner voices became stronger and stronger day by day.

I started putting my thoughts in an orderly manner and in the third week of December 2009, I made up mind to quit the firm. I told my wife and parents about it and they were prepared to sacrifice if need be, their wants and existing comforts, to accommodate my new venture. I told them that I will not look for a job elsewhere and that I am getting ready to start a firm on my own. They were shocked as they did not know how much investment was necessary to get started.

Now that I had made my decision, the next big task was to communicate the same to P.S.S.sir and I was particular that I will tell only him and no one else before I told him. At office, I was informed that Surana Sir was on travel and that he was not expected until last week of December 2009. I had to leave for my hometown with my family for Christmas vacation at least on 22-12-2009. Therefore on 21-12-2009 I wrote a detailed letter and sealed it and wrote 'confidential' on the envelope and placed it under a paper weight on Sir's table for him to find when he had returned. I left for my vacation with my family awaiting the response.

As is the usual practice till today, Surana sir called me on Christmas day of 2009 and wished me, Minu, my kids and my parents separately on my phone and finally told me that he has seen my "love letter" and that he will discuss it with me personally when I resume in January. After the Christmas vacation I returned back to Chennai and went to SSIA on 2nd January 2010. After a long exit interview with Surana Sir, I got relieved from my duties at the law firm and as a great gesture SIR himself came down to see me off after wishing me all the very best for all my future endeavors.

In first week of January after I left the firm, Amar K Panwar expressed his intention to join me as a partner in the new venture. We sat down for a lunch at Hotel Palmgrove and I told Amar the name of the firm 'Chennai Law Associates'. I also showed him the logo and the tagline 'Engineers of Law'. I had worked on it with an old neighbor Mr. Daniel John who was a printer. Instantly Amar said we will do it and suggested I speak to

K. Subhashini Suresh and her husband Mr. Suresh to know if she was willing to join the partnership. On the very same day we spoke to her and her husband Mr. Suresh also readily agreed. But I made it a point that both of them should inform Surana sir that they are going to Join me in my new venture, take his consent, get relieved and only then we can take this idea forward. I told both of them that I was willing to wait for that to happen.

Friends appear from nowhere when in real need. Ramesh Mardia was the first to stand with me during the crisis. He owns an electrical wire manufacturing and trading business and an office very close to the High Court of Madras near the State Bank of Mysore. A client facing problems in Debt Recovery Tribunal gave the first Vakalat in a Writ Petition that was filed by Chennai Law Associates. The office table and computer of Ramesh Mardia was given to me and I started Chennai Law Associates from his officeall alone. My partners were looking for an opportune moment to inform 'Sir'about their decision to leave. Meanwhile, I filed the writ petition challenging an order of the Chief Judicial Magistrate, Vellore and attended Vellore Court proceedings with the client and the Writ petition was taken up by the bench and status quo was ordered on 19-01-2010. Parallel to these activities, Subashini got relieved after properly explaininghher decision to Surana sir and we went to see an office premises opposite Bank of Baroda, a premises owned by Basic Engineers and Traders on the Second floor at Errabalu Street, Chennai. We were introduced as 'good lawyers' by Ramesh Mardia- my friend. The office furniture and minor interior works were finished by 19-01-2010 and the date was fixed for inauguration as 20-01-2010. Amar took some time to place his resignation at SSIA and after all his formalities, he too joined us in the first week of February 2010. At the same time, Sridevi a paralegal attached to SSIA expressed her intention to join CLA and Mishraji, an ex-accountant who resigned a year ago also wanted to join CLA.

Always realize and listen to your inner call and respond to it. Never compromise on your individuality. Think deep and act fast. Never sleep after you were hit by a Dream. Work on your dream. Sleep not until your dream becomes a reality. Have courage- the courage of communicating your desire and thoughts to the concerned person irrespective of the status and position of that person. It is your requirement. You have to take the initiative. If necessary wrest the initiative. There is nothing wrong. Keep your mind clear and transparent. Lead with conviction and determination. Success cannot evade you for long.

I looked at the calendar and saw that December 2009 had started and the half lent of Catholics prior to Christmas (25 days fasting) was undertaken by me too. My prayers to the Christ to be born on Christmas of 2009 were single folded – I leave Surana with my head held high and I commence my own firm without any delay at the earliest. On 23rd December 2009, I got the courage and internal message from my maker to communicate my decision at any cost that day before leaving to my native place with my wife and 2 daughters for Christmas. I was disappointed to hear that Surana Sir was travelling on that day and he was expected to return only around 3rd of January or so. I wrote a letter filled with gratitude for whatever Surana Sir had done for me and also communicated my decision to quit. I left the letter personally on Sir's table with a paper weight on it and had not told anyone in the office about it. The customary wish over phone on the Christmas day, 2009 came from Surana Sir as usual. His voice was cordial and he did not hide his disappointment at my decision. Since it was a festival and that too Christmas, perhaps Sir was not angry with me. He wanted me to discuss the matter in person when I came back to Chennai. I was asked to come as usual on 2nd January 2010. I went and after a long meeting that lasted around 3 hours, I was finally permitted to get relieved of all my duties at Surana and Surana from the next day. I still remember the grace with which Surana Sir came down to the parking lot with me and wished me good luck in all what I do and saw me off on 03.01.2010.

The next few days, I sat with my friend in his office opposite the High Court, with nothing much to do but plan and work on the already conceived law firm. I worked on the name of my firm, a logo and a tagline to describe what we intend to do in the law firm. My neighbor was a printing professional who helped me come up with decent stationary materials such as letterheads, visiting cards, envelopes, etc. Everything was ready but for the office and clients. My colleague from Surana expressed his ardent wish to join me and was meeting me during his free time in between passovers and others sessions in the High Court and DRT. The two of us later met another colleague from Surana and as requested by her, met her husband and explained about what Chennai Law Associates will be and into what role she could step in if she joins. The trio as we stand now, i.e., the 3 partners of Chennai Law Associates, came together for the first time on 10.01.2010, when we met to identify a premises for rent at the Errabalu Chetty Street in Chennai, proximate to the High Court. How much we could invest and what were the minimum requisites were the topics of discussion during the initial days. Whatever I said, be it the name of the firm, the logo, the premises for rent or anything for that matter, did not get a negative response from my partners and that by itself, was the greatest motivation to go ahead and go for it.

Amar K. Panwar is the youngest amongst the 3 partners of Chennai Law Associates. His manners, strictly religious attitude and self discipline he follows sets him a class apart amongst his peers. The expertise he possesses in debt recovery matters and his willingness to participate in criminal case proceedings and trials brought him into Chennai Law Associates (CLA) as the Head – Banking Division. His residence being the closest to our office premises, he was also hand-picked by us as the administrative head in-charge of staff leave and roll call. Amar, being the young partner amongst us, is also in-charge of our computer systems, networks within the office and all technical aspects to be maintained and looked after for proper and effective functioning of our firm. More than a partner in the firm, Amar is like a brother to me and I can confide many matters in him and he has always stood rock solid during tough times of the firm and certain financial arrangements that were required to be made overnight were done with ease whenever it mattered. The love and affection we share for each other is much more than that of natural brothers. His decade long journey with me at CLA is by itself a testimony of his goodness, loyalty and the deep relationship he is nurturing with me.

K. Subhashini was mooted to be taken as a partner of CLA by none other than Amar and the preliminary meetings we had with Subhashini at her house in the presence of her husband Mr. Suresh, who is a bank officer, were very informal. The sincerity with which Subhashini received the conversations and the eagerness she showed to quit Surana and Surana by mentioning the fact that she will be joining me at CLA show the courage and determination she had to join CLA. Her expertise on the Writ jurisdiction was effective and useful in the coming days of CLA. Subhashini's exposure in the High Court and contacts, even before she joined Surana and Surana, were revived for the greater benefit of CLA. Multitasking and seeing the game till the finish line are qualities that place her far ahead of other contemporaries of her age and experience. Her working hours of 8:30AM to 8:30PM till date, despite being a mother of 2 school going children speaks volumes about her sincerity and dedication to the profession and to CLA. As a lawyer, she has also started appearing in the Hon'ble Supreme Court of India on matters that she has handled in the High Court of Madras and there have been many meritorious cases that she has dealt with at CLA with least contribution from me and Amar. Her contribution towards CLA's success march of over a decade by now, is praiseworthy.

Chennai Law Associates was inaugurated in a simple ceremony on 20.01.2010 with the grace and wishes of Sr. Counsels Mr. AR L Sundaresan and Mr. Raghunathan, at Errabalu Chetty Street opposite the Bank of Baroda, marking the beginning of our own litigation firm, also involved in corporate consultancy and the all new entertainment law division under my leadership.

Chennai Law Associates CLA

"The ladder of success is best climbed by stepping on the rungs of opportunity."

-Ayn Rand, *Russian American Author and philosopher*

Prior to the inauguration of Chennai Law Associates, I worked on a website for the Law firm. Initially it was www.ibiremediumatcla. com, inspired by the latin maxim 'ubi jus ibiremedium' which translated to'Where there is law there is remedy'. So I decided that our website address could mean "there is remedy at CLA". But in the later years after Chennai Law Associates had made itself visible in legal circles, we decided to keep the law firm name itself as the website address and so, it is now www.chennailawassociates.com. There was not even one Vakalat or any brief in the beginning when we commenced CLA, but by June 2010 we assessed CLA and found that we had crossed 300 Vakalats in just about a week more than 5 months. It was a good going for a just born law firm by any standards. Almost 60 clients were entrusting their cases to us apart from the advisory services we were rendering during that period. Statistics showed that we had not yet taken a decision to regret and we, the partners of CLA, were extremely happy to see our efforts grow in leaps. By now we have crossed 8,500 Vakalats and have brought successful end to more than 4000 cases to the satisfaction of our clients.

At the very first Partners meeting at CLA in first week of February 2010, I insisted that we will never dilute the intensity of our Welcome Note in our website:

"At CLA, we assure our clients of quality legal services through prompt, apt and timely action so as to provide best relief in a cost effective manner.

We believe that law has to be constructively administered for achieving optimum results in the shortest possible span of time. We at CLA believe firmly that Legal Engineering can alone help us achieve this for our esteemed clients.

We firmly believe that the smile of a satisfied client is most precious recognition for the services rendered to him by CLA and each one of us at CLA will continue to strive for more and more such precious recognition, day after day.

We are therefore proud to be called Engineers of Law.

Managing Partner

M.L Joseph"

I can say with utmost humility that we as a team have till date, lived up-to the above promise given by me as the Managing Partner.

We, the partners of CLA, intended to make the CLA premises as a second home to all the staff and lawyers who are employed with us. The office has been designed in such a manner that there is more access to all the main partners for any staff member, irrespective of the hierarchy. I always believe that for any family to strengthen its bond, at least one meal a day should be had together around the dining table. For the last 10 years, not a single lunch at CLA has gone by without this practice being ceremoniously followed. I used to feel for my juniors at times, when the Court work would prolong to 3 or 3:30 PM and the young juniors would still wait to have lunch together with me even if it was to be at 4PM.

Though, such incidents occurred very rarely, maybe twice of thrice a year, the intimacy, the affection and oneness that was demonstrated is indeed laudable and I am proud of having been able to form such a wonderful CLA Family. We all eat together without any fuss and with a lot of fun and also serious case discussions, at times. Every alternate month, we find reasons to go out for a trip and have lunch or dinner outside in different restaurants and the friendship we share during such occasions make us closer by cutting the strings of any formal hierarchy that may exist due to our positions in the firm.

The firm is very clear on the exit formalities of its employees if and when they choose to leave. It is a matter of pride that very few staff and lawyers have left CLA and those who left had compelling reasons to do so. A customary lunch and positive views of all existing members about the person leaving were shared affectionately. Despite leaving CLA, each one of them remain in touch with each of us till date. I have to say that those farewell meetings were very emotional at times and the inevitability to part was the only reason the employee would have for taking such a decision. Every person who went on with different aspects of their career and family commitments are still connected and in close contact with me individually and with the firm professionally till today. To leave a mark in your employees and the staff and people who do even the smallest of errands in the office is the biggest achievement that any employer should look for and I feel satisfied that CLA has been able to do this wonderfully well so far. When it comes to work, not a single person at CLA will try to avoid it or give reasons for postponement. They would rather stay back beyond their regular timings and also offer to come on Sundays and holidays, if the work was so pressing.

Nothing was planned for the future of CLA and things unfolded naturally. Between January 2010 and September 2011, in a very short span of time we moved into a bigger office at Armenian Street with the blessings of the same landlord – Basic Engineers and Traders. The renovated office became a reality with the help of many brothers of mine, who took pride in being a part of the success story of Chennai Law Associates. Gratitude is due to Ramesh Mardia of Mardia Cables, TR Sivaraman of Classic Polo, Allwyn of Dollar Apparels, Uday Shankar of Sri Santosh Textiles and many more people who contributed financially and emotionally to make it all happen. A grand inauguration ceremony was held for the renovated office on 03.09.2011, wherein the most respected Sr. Counsels R. Krishnamoorthy, NR Chandran, Jayaraman, Raghunathan (senior most practicing lawyers of the Madras Bar) graced the occasion and offered their felicitation and wishes to CLA. Soon after the renovation of our office, news spread about Chennai Law Associates thick and fast amongst the legal circle. A special mention of Mrs. Meera Gupta, who directly joined our renovated office on 03.09.2011 needs to be placed on record. Her motherly presence at CLA and the arbitration division and practice that we intended to promote, safely rested in her hands thereafter and outstanding matters were done on the arbitration front in the years to come. She took up her position as the Director of our exclusive 'Chennai's Centre for Excellence in Arbitration' that is a part of CLA.

At CLA, I had the benefit of working with highly intellectual and young lawyers of the latest generation, fully equipped to handle technical and technological stuff. To adopt technology in legal research and to place relevant and material decisions of the Higher Courts and the Apex Court, was child's play for these youngsters as they did it with such precision and ease. Mr. Nevin Sabu, a NUALS graduate from Kochi, joined me in September 2011 and was with me until April, 2015. His grasp and conversion of my thoughts into documents at great speed was phenomenal. Towards, April 2014, yet another youngster by name AashishDafaria, a ILS Gold medalist from Pune (of Chennai origin), joined me and the outstanding contribution he made to our presence on the internet and the zeal shown by him to showcase CLA to the corporate world and to work which I personally did with him at Entertainment Law Division, interacting and coordinating with big names of Bollywood and Kollywood industry, simultaneously are fresh in my memory. RevathiDamodaran, another young post-graduate in law from School of Excellence, Chennai, was also a gold medalist in mathematics, who served CLA outstandingly well, between 2013 and 2017. Advocate Cintha from School of Excellence, Chennai and Advocate Vinu Mary Joy, also contributed significantly at CLA. The Advocates at CLA, namely Sakthivel, an engineering graduate who took on to law, Advocate Nandini Murali and Advocate A. Aravind intellectuals who contribute for the day to day progress of CLA.

By the first anniversary of CLA, we had a small team of 5 lawyers, two stenos, one paralegal and an accountant, a manager and two office assistants. We were a family of 12 members – yes CLA Family. We happily celebrated our First Anniversary recalling our achievements of the year that went by. We went to a shopping mall and spent our time together with our families and had food together and the happiness in that unity gave me an infinite happiness.

We moved on forward getting good orders from almost all the courts in Chennai and also in some matters from Bangalore, Delhi and also Kerala in the cases we handled for clients from different strata of the society. By the last week of July 2009 our landlords M/s. Basic Engineers and Traders wanted us to explore as to whether we could take a larger premises owned by them on rent and the same was on Armenian street, which was more proximate to the High Court campus and had a prominent address. Even though we were not fully ready, our dearest well-wishers, mainly from Tiruppur insisted that I should not leave this opportunity as we may not get a more appropriate office premises than this. If I call them brothers of CLA- it will not be fair enough.Indeed they are the benevolent patrons of CLA who pushed me to go for it and parted with unimaginable portions of money to help make our dream a reality. It was a paradigm shift from the 850 Sq Ft premises to the 5000 Sq Ft premises. I took pride in designing the cabins and utilities myself. Within 28 days the premises was ready for inauguration. On 9thSeptember 2011, the present office premises was inaugurated by the great senior advocates Shri. R.Krishnamoorthy sir, Shri N.R. Chandran sir, Shri Jayaraman Sir and Shri. Raghunathan sir - all of whom had completed more than 50 years of exemplary professional service in the High court of Madras in various fields of law. Legal luminaries, our friends and the clients of CLA made the event a milestone in the history of CLA. The new office had an inbuilt Arbitration Centre, a reception named 'Swagatham' a conference space called 'Vishist' a visitor's area called 'Shresht' an inter-religious prayer area called 'Sannidhi' and a dining area named 'Swad'. We wanted to continue the use of the classical terms of the Sanskrit language, which I consider has been the bridge between languages of the Northern part of India and Southern part. Thus, a grand infrastructure for CLA was in place in less than 2years and we were ready to serve corporates in the manner they wanted us to. I have to place on record the immense sacrifice of my admirable warriors - Partners of CLA - Mrs. K. Subhashini Suresh and Mr. Amar K Panwar. They treat me as their elder brother and as an integral part of their family. They have withstood my mood-swings and temperaments for more than a decade by now and always gave priority to the needs and emergent requirements of Chennai Law Associates over and above their own personal requirements and the sacrifices made by them have infused blood into the living body of CLA.

After CLA was ready with the new office, the request from Mrs. Meera Gupta was taken into the fold as a Senior Associate and made the Director of the Arbitration Centre as stated above. She is with us since then. Full freedom to work with dignity and avail the comfort of taking leave whenever she wanted and many accommodations considering her age and status in the society, are given to her at CLA in reciprocation to the motherly care which she showers on all of us till date. The happiness I see in her eyes as she ages gracefully with us is more than any precious material gift that I could get from her.

Various persons of immense talent joined CLA other than my two wonderful partners to form the TEAM. I have no doubt in stating that

CLA would not have survived for a whole decade but for their sacrifices. At CLA Family, we ensure the warmth of a true family and a culture of respect for each other. We succeeded in creating an environment of fun and the space to work individually if need be with guidance of immediate leaders –the partners. Each member of the family was a leader of different type in their own sphere of activity. We have created a sense of ownership inside the minds of each member of the family. The fun, happiness and togetherness are unique. We eat together. We play indoor games together. We read general books together once a week. We are a part of CLA family Whatsapp group which is active from 6.00 AM onwards each day. I make it a point to write a thought for the day without fail. The togetherness was also experienced by all our CLA family members who went on to make a career for themselves elsewhere at various points of time for various reasons at various times. I fondly recall the huge efforts of Mrs. Renuka Shankar, Y. Rajesh, Mr. Nevin Sabu Cherian, Mr. Ashish Dafaria, Mrs. Revathi, Mrs. Cintha, Mrs. Tamilselvi, Mrs. Vinu, Mr. RajuBhaskar, Mr. T.D. Mathew, Mr. Mishraji, Mrs. Lalitha, Mrs. Vijayalakshmi, Mr. Raju, Mr. Prabhu, Mr. Kumar, Mr. Kuralarasan, and Mr. Ramadoss. I express my heartfelt thanks for all their selfless efforts and contributions put in by them during their tenure at CLA.

It is hard to believe that CLA has crossed 10 wonderful years and has many achievements to its name by now. I am proud to have been the founder of this wonderful family and I am extremely happy to get excellent comparative feedback from the young interns who visit and work with us to train for short periods, comparing their experiences in other law firms. The affection and interaction of the leaders here with the interns makes CLA so special to one and all, who enter CLA.

Be cordial to everyone. A smile - it costs nothing. We are humans. We need our space and time to do work. Constant monitoring and pestering for completion of work may not get the desired results. Watching from a distance and subtle supervision is what works all the time. To bring a sense of guilt in not completing the work efficiently will never motivate the employee. To be with them in the process of learning, guiding them without accusations, owning the responsibility when the attempt fails so as to relieve juniors of the pain and burden of the loss, are some practical methods of leadership put into use by me at CLA to make it a success machine. Building relationships with persons filled with values is the best thing you can do. Don't worry about the investment that takes to build such long lasting relationships.

An academic climate and a warm and friendly approach for discussions and the encouragement to write articles on law and a home away from home, continues to be the specialty of CLA, even today. I wish it remains this way for the rest of the time as well.

New Looks And Wider Reach - (C L A-Laurels)

"Great things are not done by impulse, but by a series of small things brought together."

Chennai Law Associates was being discussed in the High Court corridors in two Special Cases that brought distinct attraction to the Firm on the Litigation front in 2011-2012. The agriculturists on the stretch of Noyyal River grouped themselves and had commenced litigation against all Fabric Dyeing Units from in and around Tiruppur and in small towns of the river banks. Their case was against the uncontrolled water pollution that was being unleashed on to the river water and ground water due to these Dyeing Units. The case had invited earlier orders of regulations and strict implementation of Zero Liquid Discharge (ZLD) norms so far as all these dyeing units are concerned and compensation by the state from the fines levied and collected from the erring units. These orders were flouted by most of the dyeing units and the HIGH COURT of MADRAS ordered closure of all dyeing units at one stroke. Some of the genuine units who were following the ZLD norms to perfection got adversely affected. One such company which was also a giant in the manufacture of Men's apparel from Tiruppur, had dyeing units that were following the liquid discharge procedure in letter and spirit and were carrying on the activity with 100% compliance of all legalities. The company had sufficiently documented its compliances from time to time and therefore we approached the High Court to order a court appointed commissioner to inspect the unit and after the court being satisfied with the compliance of ZLD, the company was permitted to commence its operations as earlier without any change. I must recall the presence of the Managing Director Mr. T. Gopal – Royal Classic Mills Pvt Ltd., in CLA continuously for about 5 days during the said period. We were the first to open the dyeing unit after satisfying the compliance of all norms imposed by the Tamil Nadu Pollution Control Board and the Hon'ble High Court of Madras. The television channels carried news reports of this achievement. This led us to several other companies in Tiruppur and we could get favorable orders for all those who approached us in the process highlighting the necessity to follow ZLD and some companies ensured the same by procuring filters and equipment with advanced technology from Germany.

Yet another case which earned lot of attraction for Chennai Law Associates was a case related to the challenge of a Sale Deed Executed by a Public Charitable Trust allegedly violating the Scheme suit to which the trust was a party and by alleged manipulating the court permission without taking the consent of all the trustees of the Trust. After the initial round of challenge before the Single Judge, the matter was taken up before the Division Bench on day to day basis and several Senior counsels appeared for the case. During the hearing dates of that case, the hearing would takemost part of the whole day and lawyers who had cases listed in the said court would whisper to others in the corridor, 'that Chennai law associates case will take the entire day, no need to wait,'. Despite the wait caused to them, it was indeed a proud moment that within a year of its existence CLA had stamped a mark for itself as being one among the top litigation Law Firms in the Madras High court and the reach and results were indeed overwhelming.

After the renovated office started functioning, the top officials of the Japanese giant KOBELCO who had their manufacturing facility in SRI

CITY on the outskirts of Chennai(yet in Andhra Pradesh), visited us and we inked a retainer agreement for all their day to day advisory services and over time more companies including HYUNDAI GLOVIS signed their retainer agreements with CLA.

Some of the extremely satisfying moments of rendering spectacular legal services to the needy by CLA are as under:

i.   CLA handled a pro-bono case for two spinster sisters of 40 plus age in Chennai. They were being harassed by their Landlord to vacate their rented house and the case was in the Rent ControlCourt at Chennai. Within two years of the case we were able to drive sense into the landlord who agreed to waive eighteen months rent and returned the security advance which was sufficient for these two spinsters to move out into a better place for slightly higher rent. Though there was absolutely no fees collected from these poor unmarried sisters, the moral satisfaction that each member of CLA derived in getting such a huge relief making a substantial change in their life, is unparalleled.

ii. A lad who was washing cars in our neighborhood, who I used to help for with his college education fees as well, approached me with his mother one day at home (he was also washing my car daily early in the morning). When she met me, his mother started weeping profusely. She sadly expressed that her daughter's married life was being wasted due to the hurried marriage which they arranged without proper verification of the groom. Her daughter's husband was impotent and the condition was irreversible. The marriage had taken place seven months prior to that day. She wanted a legal separation and the cost of marriage that they incurred as compensation. CLA put all its efforts and a Decree of Nullity was obtained within four months. The husband returned the marriage expenses as claimed by the wife's parents and thereafter we were invited for the girl's second marriage after six months. She is happily married and has a boy child now. The immense satisfaction we derive from such social causes of being there for the needy when it matters makes a big difference to our purpose as a legal professional. It generates enormous goodwill which are truly silent bank deposits.

iii. One of our clients is a reputed seller of Milk Sweets and Bakery products in Chennai and wanted to purchase a property. The property was under litigation. The dispute was pending in the High Court. The case was regarding probating a will and the fight was between 21 family members, some settled here in Chennai and some in the US and other foreign countries. The property was appropriate for our client and he wanted to purchase it. Amongst 21 litigants there were three camps out of which two camps were so inimical that they refused to see eye to eye. I organized several meeting with these people of different camps and our client and lawyers of opposing parties and after several round of negotiation a joint compromise was executed between parties. Our client got the property by way of different sale deeds from litigating parties for valuable sale consideration and all was well in the end. A litigation of 17 years prior to that was put an end by time bound and timely action at CLA.

iv. My friendship with ace director N. Lingusamy and his brother through a friend and junior advocate Maruti Thulasidharan grew thick and fast after CLA was formed. From 2010-2015 there was opportunity to defend many litigations for the production house owned by the Ace Director and his brothers. From Paiyya to Rajini Murugan, the film releases were more thrilling than the films themselves. The work done by me personally on account of my friendship with the troubled production house and the alert and effective team work at CLA by my peers and juniors gave tremendous relief to the client. I can safely and proudly say that the work done at Chennai Law associates was a major factor that contributed the release of Paiyaa, ManjaPai, VazhakkuEnn 18/9, Anjaan, SathurangaVettai, Kumki, Ivan Vera Mathiri, Vettai, Uthama Villain and RajiniMurugan. So much work was done in court by us for 'RajiniMurugan' that a reputed Judge who has recently become a Supreme court Judge said in open court, 'serve papers on Chennai Law Associates and get them next day as they are the lawyer for the production house', in a case where the petitioner moved against our client and our client's appearance was yet to be effected. We appeared, gained time and worked out a settlement that later on saw the release of the said film. Chennai Law Associates gained immense popularity during these days.

v.   I must admit that post 2014 there were outstanding cases that werehandled without my involvement by Advocate K. Subhashini, wherein she fought a pro-bono case completely on her own and secured the Job of Sub-Inspector of Police for a candidate who had lost his father and there was allegation of recording the chest expansion of the said candidate wrongly to disqualify him in the Physical Examination. In the writ petition filed by CLA on his behalf, reexamination was ordered to be done in the presence of the Registrar General of the High Court of Madras and appropriate orders passed to complete his physical and medical examination and the said person is now employed as a Sub Inspector of Police in Tamil Nadu Police.

vi.   Similarly to the credit of CLA was yet another case where a student got a medical seat in the Krishnagiri Government Medical College after tremendous efforts on the writ jurisdiction was put in with regard to NEET anomalies in the year 2015 and the student's admission was secured in 2016. Not a single word of pleading was dictated by me nor was my appearance in court necessitated in this case too. This gave me a lot of freedom as the firm was in safe hands even in my absence. While serious litigation was taken care by the experienced lawyer / partner, all the administration works and court management for the day was well taken care of by Amar KPanwar.

vii.   Another memorable compromise that was actively mooted by me was in an Intellectual property litigation that was almost 14 years old and had faced several rounds at various levels of the judiciary and was now before the IPAB- New Delhi- then presided over by His Lordship Mr. Justice K.N. Basha. With some agreeable changes to our clients mark much to the satisfaction of our client as well, the US garment and fashion giant agreed to close all litigation against our client and an appropriate Memo of Compromise was executed and filed in the IPAB and orders communicated to Civil court and Trade mark Registry where certain proceeding between the same parties on the same trade mark were pending back then.

viii. In 2016, Chennai Law Associates under the able leadership of K. Subhashini, took up another case for the social cause. Engineering Diploma holders selected by Chennai Metro Rail Corporation were not being given their appointment orders and there was an attempt to appoint contract workers in their place. Effective orders in Writ Petition, Writ Appeal, Contempt Jurisdiction and also Special leave Petition were obtained in favor of these rural poor educated youth who will now get employed in the Chennai Metro Rail Corporation which was possible in such a short time by herculean efforts undertaken at CLA.

ix.   Many deserving cases of poor and neglected women facing severe cruelty and domestic violence from their husband and his relatives were undertaken by CLA on cost basis most of the times without charging any professional fees, more as a contribution towards alleviating their miseries.

x. In the second week of December 2019, a man in his 30s walked into my office just by seeing the sign board downstairs. By telling his story he was profusely weeping. He said his current high court lawyer died recently. I kept him there and verified the same. It was true. He was convicted by the trial court for Dowry Death, since his wife committed suicide within 7 years of their marriage. The Criminal appeal against the said conviction was being listed in the High Court of Madras when the said counsel had died. Recording the conduct of the husband at the time of the incident and several earlier incidents of the wife deserting the husband and the husband giving police complaint to get his wife back to live with him etc., which were amply available in evidence with the trial court records, a judgment reversing his conviction was granted by the Hon'ble High Court. I took just a week for presenting my arguments in the High Court and the relief obtained was felt so immensely by the poor man.

There are several such success stories lying in the records chest at Chennai Law Associates, all satisfying stories of people, who got justice for their cause and of lawyers who worked for justice and achieved the balance. All these were against all odds, with the sole cause - the social cause, in mind.

Delegation And Time Management

"Either you run the day or the day runs you."

-Jim Rohn, *American Entrepreneur, author and motivational speaker*

S ome of the great lessons that I learnt practically in my career thus far which have contributed in a big way to my success so far are summarized in this chapter for easy reference of the younger generation.

Managing time on any given day is the key to success in any field. The conservative method of making a 'To-do' list by manually writing it down in a note book with dates and taking a look at clearing those tasks one by one is by far the most effective deterrent of falling back. Before closing the day's work it is necessary to carry forward unaccomplished tasks to the next day's list. Next day, new tasks can be added to the list prepared the previous night and a comprehensive list can be made once again. Time to make this list will not exceed 10 minutes. It is not necessary to do the first in the list first. Whatever from the list can be done can be attempted and done and struck off physically. It is the unexpected work that springs upon us that derails our existing work. Prioritizing our work on urgency and importance has pushed the regular tasks behind and they remain unfinished even now. These are regular excuses given by most of us when we are reminded of a normal work that ought to have been completed long ago. Most of us do not have super memory and we are not machines to perform with the same level of consistency each time.

Second and most important aspect of time management is to practice speedier response to emails in your inbox. Do not allow accumulation of emails in your inbox. Do whatever is possible to give a reply as soon as possible. Prompt response makes anyone happy and satisfied, be it your client or your acquaintance. It shows your alertness and care to the person and issue raised in the email. It is a main mark of professionalism. If the query raised requires a detailed response with a little more research on the subject, intimate the same to the querist with a fair estimate of response time. Stick to the timeline and give your detailed response within the extended time. Seeking another extension of time gain will show your incompetence or laziness. Handle each enquiry with care, big or small. Don't pre-determine the significance or insignificance of the matter without making any efforts to understand the issue. Sometimes issues which you assessed to be small in the beginning will be very serious and grave as you step into facts and one small fact may lead you to a bigger fact and more important one and vice versa. Do not ignore any instruction of your client as irrelevant. Clear your inbox (both in your laptop and in your mind) ASAP and be ready to take more work every single day.

My senior always highlighted the importance of working fast and doing active power drafting within a given time and pushing the draft for finalization and achieving a faster filing of a case entrusted in the office, without compromising on the quality of the drafts. Coming to office as the first person and refusing to go even when the office has to be closed can never be the index of hard work or loyalty or capacity to perform. Smart work was always stressed by him as the need of the hour. 'I don't need buffalos and donkeys in my office", proclaimed my erstwhile senior, "I need tigers and leopards and panthers who are active and smart in their work."

Time management is often coupled with the art of delegation. Yes delegation of work is by itself an art. The choice of right person for the right job is the first rule that can make delegation successful at work. Just imagine a wrong person being delegated with a work that could have been otherwise done by you. The work will be erratically performed and it will require a redo. Such careless delegation would result in enormous wastage of time and will act as the worst enemy of your time management skills. To effectively delegate you must know the skills and interests and inclination of the resources available at your disposal. To assess the strengths and weaknesses of your human resources, you should spend time informally with your down-line members in a random manner over a period of time. Spending time with your team socially yet keeping a distance from their personal side is the balancing act that should be undertaken to achieve the purpose of fair assessment of your team members.

Most and more at work can be practiced with the help of time management only. Time management can be effectively practiced only by invoking delegation of work to the best abilities of the team inter se. What to delegate and what not to, is also very important. For example, sometimes a client with utmost faith on the senior at the office comes with a relatively smaller issue that can very well be handled by the junior counsel at office. However the client is very close to the firm and from what he says he wants the senior to attend to. A careful hearing can be given to the client's needs in the presence of the junior without disclosing the purpose of the junior in that discussion. If possible the client can be relieved with information about when his work will be completed by you. Thereafter the work can be done by the junior counsel and after a personal check of the work being satisfactorily done, the same can be delivered to the client within the time specified.

For effective implementation of quality time management tools and enhancing the art of delegation, one must constantly educate and train his work-force. Only if the leader in you has confidence in the person to whom the work is delegated can the work be done effectively in lesser time than it would have originally consumed. Just as we teach our younger ones cycling we need to hold the trainee for some time when they practice cycling. Then walk with them as they cycle making them feel that we are holding the cycle and then slowly watch from a short distance and rush to their rescue if they were losing balance on the cycle. Despite all these acts of care and caution, the trainee will fall off the cycle unexpectedly. Sometime they will be slightly injured too. Even the cycle can be slightly damaged. It doesn't matter. The object is to teach the younger ones the skills of cycling. So long as we achieve this objective, there is no great loss in these small injuries and minor damages to the cycle. It is therefore important that we travel with the person for a considerable time, before effectively delegating important work to them.

Make one person responsible for the work and let that person alone report to you on the work any time you call for the status of work. Make it clear that the said person need not do it by himself. He can very well delegate it further with a close watch on the developments in that work. Teach your junior colleagues also the art of effective delegation and yet hold them responsible specifically for the execution of the job in hand.

Time management of the individual in you and the team led by you are important separately and jointly. The time efficiency of the team may lag due to ineffective delegation and wrong assessment of required time for a particular job. Every part of the job should be completed within a time frame with the available resources. Constant review of progress of the work entrusted/ delegated without disturbing the work should help in expediting closure time.

Mere existence on this earth for longer time will not be deemed as experience for a person practicing any profession, more so for a lawyer. Experience means going through a set of facts or a case intellectually and by involving yourself in the work of that case until its final verdict, whether favorable or unfavorable. Both results will enhance your experience for sure. That is why the profession of law is termed as a 'practice'. Your day, week, month and year being effectively subjected to proper time management as above and repeating it as a habit consistently will enable you to condense more work into less number of years and will make you overtake the experience of lawyers who do not do so. Every young lawyer should value time as the most precious commodity and try to associate himself with the knowledgeable crowd and spend quality time in skill acquisition by doing as much work as possible in short span of time and thereafter once confident of the experience gained, move on to wisely delegate the works that can be delegated to the right person and start doing multiple works at several stages simultaneously. That is the scientific way to grow in the practice of law. I know many elderly advocates who have enrolled themselves as lawyers even before I was born, but I cannot say that they have practiced the profession of law in the right earnest as suggested hereinabove.

However, it is also important that while doing all this effectively, never forget to take a break at the right time. When you feel stretched to the maximum and you feel you should take rest. Just shut down your laptop and switch off your mind and sleep if possible for thirty minutes irrespective of the time of the day. The refreshed mind after the sleep will be productive multifold than the tired one before the break.

Effective delegation of your work is crucial for time management. Manage your time wisely. Way to go.

Client Management

"A customer is the most important person in your premises".

- Mahatma Gandhi, *Father of our nation*

Aclient is valuable. He feeds us with knowledge and resources for our survival. Infact our lifestyle enhancements are possible only because of them. I remember those olden days when my senior used to adopt techniques of 'BOSSING' at all levels. When I say all levels I mean it - verbal, physical and emotional transgression was permissible those days. The clients realised that they were in the company of a very big Senior, when the juniors around him looked far less competent than the senior, intellectually and capacity wise. Invariably, all the seniors of that period were behaving inhumanly according to various junior advocates of different law firms and specialised camps of practice of law under the leadership of their respective able and experienced seniors. I have no hesitation in saying that I too am a product of the old school method of learning, which did not spare the cane to spoil the child.

Clients were also not treated in red-carpet style with tea and snacks as we now do. They had to wait for hours after reporting to the senior-most-junior or even better placed clerks in the office, who had access to the senior advocate-perhaps the only decision maker in the office at any point of time irrespective of the senior's mood. Clients were willing to wait for senior's free and uninterrupted time sometimes for weeks together with money in their hand. Junior advocates can take instructions from the client only with the permission of the Senior Counsel but were never allowed to advice without his knowledge.

Over the last twenty five years I have seen a remarkable change in the mindset of people, be it clients, senior advocates, junior advocates and the entire legal fraternity for that matter.

Firstly let me list the changes in Clients. Clients are now more aware of their legal rights and remedies than ever before. The rapid advancement of information technology and the wide electronic coverage of all the legal developments in courts throughout the country and the wide internet access to the general public have made our clients far different from the clients who were being handled by our former seniors. Clients have the choice of comparing the efficiency of their lawyers by accessing what exactly their lawyers are doing in courts by checking the case reports available on various e-libraries over internet. Age and experience of the senior has become an irrelevant factor for clients nowadays. Clients are willing to go with young brains who pass their assessment test during the email exchanges or conversation they have with their proposed counsel during their initial conversation itself. Clients are conscious of the time that can be normally consumed for a case like that of theirs. A lawyer who suggests lesser time to get them the remedy and gives confidence in a logical and methodical manner alone can impress the new breed of clients. Therefore there is a huge demand for a 'New breed of Lawyers'. Newer strategies and faster relief oriented tactful approaches if projected, can get the desired attractive professional fees as the present day's client wants to save his time which is much more precious than the extra money claimed by the New Breed of Lawyers who can deliver speedier Justice. There is a huge space wide open if you can adapt to new techniques and acquire sufficient skill to deal with the client who is highly demanding. That is precisely the reason why we often hear, 'Cranky client he is', 'Demanding Client', 'client's expectation is sky high, 'etc., from many lawyers nowadays. Inability to handle an intelligent and demanding client is due to the basic reason of our refusal to upgrade to the necessities of the ever changing legal profession.

Secondly, Senior Advocates are shedding their untouchable attitude towards learning and adapting to the newer technologies, accustoming themselves to modern practices, etc., and I have seen some Senior Advocates far ahead in comparison with the most tech savvy Junior counsel around his office. Senior counsel have started explaining to their clients what they propose to do and what exactly law says at least briefly nowadays if clients want to hear directly from the horse's mouth. It was unthinkable twenty five years ago. Clients are being advised properly by Senior advocates through their briefing counsel to take proper appointments if they intend to meet the senior advocate. At times the briefing counsel and the Senior advocate meet prior to the clients scheduled meeting to take stock of the case contents, status of the hearing in court, legal research done in the case and the possible orders that can be lawfully obtained from the court etc., to fit into the exercise of 'Home work'. A more thorough preparation of the case is seen nowadays, with dynamic participation of intelligent lawyers. A well researched and fully prepared young lawyer can win the case against any Senior counsel on a given date is also one of the reason for such a welcome attitudinal change in some Advocates who were part of a totally different school of practice.

Thirdly and most importantly is the steady inflow of well groomed young lawyers who have taken up LAW as a career not as a matter of chance but as a matter of their passion and choice. The enhanced syllabus and the focused legal education in the recent past and the serious younger generation who step into the practice of law are good reasons to be proud of the younger generation of lawyers who will never compromise on dispensing real justice to the needy, with the promise of building a nation with a strong justice delivery system. Using the mobile phones and laptops for legal research to the maximum and getting the necessary case laws to the point in shortest span of time, at times between the pre lunch session and post lunch session during the hearing of an ongoing case is in fact praiseworthy. The energy and passion to learn is seen much more in the present youngsters than the past set of young lawyers, I must say. But I must rush to add that the former junior lawyers were more open to criticism and were able to take the cussing words of a senior at times, in the right perspective. A junior advocate in the present has to be nurtured emotionally, intellectually and personally. It is important for Senior Advocates to appreciate the efforts of the young lawyer in person and in public then and there even if a small achievement was done by the junior. To keep them inspired and motivated is a must. The senior can very well spring surprises during the arguments by striking a special point deviating from the prepared notes and mock arguments which the Junior advocates were part of, and taking a new and sudden detour from the set questionnaire when the witness is in the box and achieve some good piece of oral evidence being recorded in the trial of a case, so as to stamp the mastery and authority of the Senior Counsel on the Subject. Nothing wrong in such an approach and in fact that makes the junior extra vigilant during the trial of the case or arguments being addressed by the Senior Advocate. Invariably every Lawyer's office has a Whatsapp group and Facebook page. Due credits must be given to the respective junior advocates then and there in these social media groups and make them proud. At the same time junior advocates also expect an individual appreciation directly from the senior himself.

A to Z of client management is as under:

a) Give time to your client and never waste your client's time.

b) Get organised more-so with time management and train your team to organise timely appointments and make them realise the need for sticking to the schedule.

c) Do not always depend on juniors to work on your email and laptop. Irrespective of your age arm yourself with advanced technologies.

d) Stay connected on electronic media with your team every single day.

e) Learn and teach. Don't hesitate to learn from Juniors on the go as they are indeed capable of doing effective legal research in short time. Do spend your time unhesitatingly to teach your juniors and explain to them the progress of the case and the importance of specific stand or defence taken in a particular situation of the case and make them understand how the particular effort will help decide the case by the Judge finally.

f) Explain the client the possibilities of worst situation in given circumstances. At the same time ensure that you do not press the panic button and give an impression that they are engaging a pessimist lawyer.

g) Place his strengths and weaknesses and openly discuss the law on the subject briefly with the client about the realistic remedies that are achievable from courts.

h) Train your team to perform efficiently.

i) Motivate the team using technology by sending forwards and legal developments in the work group over Whatsapp or any other social media.

j) Change old methods and implement new and effective ways of learning as a team.

k) Be a leader in all fronts. A true leader gets more success than a BOSS.

l) Educate your team and conduct periodic team exercise to understand the capacity of each member without any specific agenda.

m) Let the client see you and your team work on his case. Earlier the client was only informed about the outcome of his case. Now it is seen that the client can very well be made known of the team efforts that are put in his case.

n) Be mindful of the clients' food requirements if he is in your office during lunch time and ensure that you take care and are hospitable to them.

o) Get attached to the cause of the client and make the client feel you are indeed his well wisher.

p) If there is no need to litigate explain the same and advise the client accordingly and convince him to stay away from litigation.

q) Make the client feel important and listen to the client even if he is elaborating unnecessarily.

r) Tell the juniors to work then and there if possible in the presence of the client, so as to make him feel that your team has sufficient intellect and power to handle the situation on warfooting if need be.

s) By and large try and dictate and get the pleading or representation typed in the presence of the client. He can contribute on factual aspects then and there. Approval of the drafts can be done instantaneously and delay in execution of the work can be avoided.

t) Give an upfront transparent scope of work and estimate of fees and expenses to the best of your ability so that proper justification for the proposed costs that the client has to incur can be justified at any point of time later.

u) Client should be informed roughly the necessity of number of expected personal appearances in the court so as to plan their work and business effectively.

v) An adverse order or an unexpected set back should be communicated by the senior most Counsel who handled the case and not the junior most.

w) Remedial measures and appellate procedures to overcome the setback should be communicated to the client. Personal discussions must be held with the client without any delay so as to retain the confidence and belief of the client in you and your team.

x) Written report and communication of developments should be promptly made to the client through SMS, Whatsapp, email etc.,

y) Regular feedback from clients should be obtained through emails, personal conversation and through telephone.

z) Accommodate the client in a humane way if he wants some time for making payment or postponement in the fee schedule, as long as it is clear that your service is a paid one and not free.

The above tips are illustrative and not exhaustive by any standards. Team building and working on improving the efficiency of the team are directly linked to Client Satisfaction. I have tried to put almost all these into practice at Chennai Law Associates and therefore it did not take much time to list them down for the benefit of the young lawyers amongst the readers in you.

"Building a good customer experience does not happen by accident. It happens by design."

-Clare Muscutt,
Customer Experience Entrepreneur

Case Management

"We are what we repeatedly do. Excellence, then, is not an act, but a habit."

-Aristotle, *Greek Philosopher and polymath*

Case management is a vast subject and requires an Eagle eye view of the entire case even before filing the necessary pleadings at the initial stage. My experience in Criminal Law during the initial part of my career before moving on to Civil cases at Bangalore and Writ cases, Company Petitions, Appeals in the High court and even some cases in the Hon'ble Supreme Court has enabled me to state with confidence that customization of our skills can enable us to practice in multiple fields of law and jurisdictions.

Maintenance of the case file is the first most important aspect of case management. A glance at the outer docket of the case file should disclose the developments of the case on previous dates and for what purpose the case is posted on the next date of hearing. It is equally important to organise segmented storing of these files and a specific area of storage being allotted for different courts/case types, category wise. Specific space for *next week* case files needs to be marked. A responsible paralegal staff or junior advocate should be instructed to organize the upcoming week's cases on the last working day of each week. Proper weekly allotment of cases must be made on the last working day of the week, giving sufficient time for juniors to prepare for their respective allotted cases in advance.

These exercises must be repeated every week. The allotment must be kept undisturbed, as far as possible, during the week. If allotment is changed, the alternative is to be ensured well ahead to avoid last minute chaos and possible Non-Representation.

Case management techniques (illustrative and practical-not claimed as exhaustive) are mostly common to all the courts. Some of the most important principles of Case Management are categorized as A to Z as under:

a) Not a single case should go unrepresented in any court.

b) Proper training to junior advocates and associates inculcating the importance of representation on every hearing must be imparted.

c) Clients should be intimated through SMS/ Whatsapp/Email well in advance, regarding their presence in the court, if required.

d) If any filings need to be done on the hearing date in open court, the same should be kept ready and duly signed and stitched according to the local customs of that particular court to avoid a last minute blur.

e) If filing has to be done in the court registry, do it well in advance and ensure that the filed papers reach the court bundle for proper progress of the case on the next hearing date.

f) Preferably send a junior advocate who worked on the draft and research on case laws for the respective hearings of the said case, so as to enhance better understanding of the progress of the case, in individual and team interest.

g) Make a follow up register or record that shows all the cases handled by the team with details of the advocate who attended the case, development in court and next date and stage of the case. Ensure that the proceedings entered finally in the register are the proper adjudications recorded by the Judge in the Court docket and as reflected in the online case update portal (E-Court) rather than the oral observations heard in Court, to avoid untoward confusion. The day's proceeding chart can be circulated in the team Whatsapp group for information to the entire team and easy reference.

h) Entrust a particular paralegal staff or junior to promptly communicate the developments of the case to the client and for what purpose the case is posted to the next hearing date.

i) Plan the senior advocate's appearances in court well in advance and be ready to face the court with all relevant materials at least two days ahead. Final preparations should be concluded the previous day.

j) Instruct all concerned that they cannot leave office unless the day's work is completed as the next day's performance of the team in court will be adversely impacted.

k) Inform the gist of your efforts in writing to the client from time to time so that the client is aware of the efforts being made by the team.

l) Always prepare **Written Arguments** whether it is arguments on interim application or final arguments in the case. The Written Arguments should contain reference to brief facts, evidence that is recorded and documents marked/relied on (as the case maybe), question of law in the matter, case laws from High courts and Supreme court directly on the matter as far as possible, defence of the opposite parties, explanation on the non-applicability of the defence to the present case or vice versa, relief claimed in the case or why the case should be dismissed, if the prayer has to be moulded differently, etc. and any other relevant materials that need consideration of the court.

m) Keep the case bundle safe and well maintained with all the hearing dates duly recorded and initialed with date by the advocate who attended the case.

n) Ensure that the filed papers are docketed with title of pleading and stitched, connected loose papers to be tagged and attached to a thick docket sheet. Bundle should not contain loose papers.

o) Preferably use a proper covered flat file which has waterproof outer cover and a descriptive card indicating the case details and court where the case is pending.

p) Take the summons, notices and processes ordered by the court in time. Huge delays normally occur during service of summons in every case. This also includes the Affidavit of Service in civil cases which has to be filed on time, prior to the next hearing date, after serving notice to the Respondents or Defendants as the case may be. Carelessness at this stage by advocates and clerks can lead to unnecessary delay of months and years.

q) Communicate bad or adverse orders as soon as possible to the Senior Advocate dealing with the case. Encourage juniors to communicate adverse orders / judgments without any fear or embarrassment.

r) Prompt filing of copy applications for obtaining orders should be ensured, as the limitation period will be breached if the copy application has not been filed on time.

s) File caveats in higher courts after obtaining successful orders if there is a possibility for the other side to get stay order by filing appeal against a successful order you obtained.

t) Inform the client of costs and possibilities to win in the appeal and also ask the client frankly if he intends to engage the services of any other lawyer for appeal.

u) If, yes, take a proper letter of acknowledgment of receipt of all documents regarding his case and the reference of copy application or receipt of certified copy of the Judgment/order copy etc. and the most important declaration of no claims against the lawyer in any manner whatsoever.

v) Once these important documentations are completed, hand over all papers in a file duly indexed and arranged in a chronological order of developments in court, for the new Lawyer to take over the matter to the next stage.

w) Change of Vakalat and change of counsel should be done amicably with clients without any quarrel on financial matters particularly.

x) It can be made clear that as a matter of policy, the firm would not re-accept the case if *Change of Counsel* is opted, after some time if the client is again dissatisfied with his new choice of counsel, except under extremely special circumstances such as the death of the subsequent counsel etc.

y) Cooperate with the client and new counsel if need be for one or two hearing dates if requested by them without any extra cost to client if the change of counsel is opted during the pendency of the case.

z) Talk to the client about the sincere efforts taken in his case by your team and make him understand that you are not at fault or apologise if there has been a genuine mistake and assure him to rectify the error at your cost, if it was caused due to negligence by any member of your team. If he is unwilling to listen and persists then let him have his say completely before he leaves. But at any cost do not delay in handing over the case papers as mentioned above, but with proper NOC and consent Vakalats.

Power of Extensive Research in Case Management:

Recently in a case at the Madras High court, I was representing an unregistered partnership firm in a money suit and the law was settled that a suit by an unregistered partnership cannot be maintained. The application to reject the plaint filed by the defendants was being adjourned upon our request time and again. Finally I came across a case law from the Hon'ble Supreme court, well past midnight from the general search on 'Google' and from other e-libraries later on, that such restrictions on unregistered partnership firm cannot prevent its statutory rights or common law remedy. Also it is well settled law that part of a Plaint cannot be rejected and that the plaint has to be rejected in full if the applicant was entitled to it on merits. I had a case, a weak case with a bleak possibility of maintaining the suit, since part cause of action admittedly arose from dishonor of a cheque of the defendant for which cheque dishonor case was pending in Magistrate court and the common law remedy of injunction against the release of the a Tamil film was part of the original cause of action wherein the defendant paid a portion of the suit claim for releasing the picture. This time, to the surprise of the advocate for the Defendant, I did not ask time and I said, 'ready', when the case was called. The arguments were heard in open court and order dictated then and there by the Learned Judge giving valid and cogent reasons for dismissing the application to reject the plaint as against an unregistered partnership firm—a rare order – I must say.

The above practical suggestions will be very useful for beginners who desire to practice litigation side of Legal Practice. The golden rules mentioned above are being practiced religiously by me for the past 25 years. I have benefited immensely from disciplining my case records and behaviour on the lines of the above checklist and therefore decided to make it part of this book intended for the benefit of every young practicing lawyer who reads this book.

Self Management

"All successes begin with self-discipline. It starts with you."

-Dwayne "The Rock" Johnson, American-Canadian Actor, Motivational Speaker, producer and businessman.

Managing one's self is the most difficult task. It is certainly easier said than done. The values that have been inculcated in you are priceless and always come to the fore to your benefit. Being honest in your approach and action will fetch you tremendous goodwill in the profession. Honesty is a prime virtue that needs to be inculcated and nurtured all through. Even though I have enumerated the 5Ps as important values for a lawyer, honesty can never be considered as the least or last in the list.

Punctuality: I rate punctuality as the top value one must possess and practice as nothing is more precious than time. Not only must you ensure that you do not waste your own time but also that you do not waste the time of your clients. I have seen the casual approach that we as community have towards honoring our time commitments. Excuses are common and punctuality is very rare. To be present at a particular time for a particular event involves the time quotient of other participants as well. I rate punctuality as the top value one should possess and practice unto death. Nothing is more precious than time. If an appointment is given to a client for a particular time at your office or anywhere else, first ensure you are available and ready at least five minutes before the scheduled time. Plan accordingly well ahead during the day so that you are not late. Stick to your time commitment. Assuming there is no communication from the client even after ten minutes of your waiting, inform the client over phone or through text message that you are waiting for the scheduled appointment. If he doesn't respond then carry on with your other schedule of work. If he turns up later, please ask him to wait until you complete the ongoing work or at least for a short while wherein you can organize the present work and accommodate the client. Make the client realize that it was he who missed out on punctuality. In order to enable you to take a strong stand, you should earn a reputation that you are a person who values punctuality. To achieve this you need to plan each moment of yours cleverly and as perfect as possible. Prompt and honest communication with your clients on the rare occasions when you are unable to meet the promised timeline, will enhance your reputation for sure. Give sufficient time between your appointments for the day and do not cramp your activities. Do not agree to do more than you can actually take. Your personal time should be kept aside clearly while you plan your work. It is not a good practice to give personal reasons even rarely to justify you not being punctual. Have the courtesy to inform your client regarding postponement or cancellation of an appointment in all possible ways much before the person embarks on his journey to meet you. Therefore keep up your time commitments. Be on time to courts as well. Don't make the court wait for you, no matter how prominent you are. Straying away from punctuality is a cardinal sin in professional matters.

Planning: Have a plan. Work on the plan for sufficient time before jumping into execution. The alternate should be ready if the first plan fails. So have two or three choices, more so in cases of Litigation. Choose the least expensive and most effective one for the client, to start with. Don't go for all available legal processes at once. Plan a multi pronged attack. Launch each attack carefully and at the apt time. Timing is the key in many such attacks.

Perseverance: Perseverance is another virtue to be practiced systematically. Your hard-work can inspire a whole lot, even without your knowledge. The fruits of labour are fulfillment and happiness. Even in extremely difficult cases, there has been a breakthrough just on the strength of research. Nothing is more effective than burning the midnight oil. Fruits of labour are success and sense of pride when the unachievable becomes achievable. Perseverance is definitely a key to success. Work at it in depth for a longer time and some doors are bound to open when you thought there was none.

Physical Appearance: Your appearance matters. A proper hairdo is a must. Neat and clean clothes and robes speak volumes about the self discipline you practice. When I say neat and clean, I am conscious enough to say only that much and it need not be interpreted as expensive, rich, lavish etc., The neck band which lawyers wear as part of their robes is the piece of attire that distinguishes a lawyer from the para-legal staff. I have noticed many lawyers giving the least importance to this aspect of their attire and few others extremely particular of clean neck bands when they appear in courts. These are worn mostly when lawyers appear in court. Please ensure that you look professional and dressed appropriately from head to toe, for a court hearing. Courts are considered to be temples of justice and on most occasions, the last resort of civilised men to find a just solution through established legal system of our country. So the respect that each lawyer should bestow on the institution is expected to be of possible best standards. Dress well.

Positive Reputation: Earn the Positive Reputation or good will amongst your clients and also amongst colleagues and lawyers who appear for the other side. Above all earn the goodwill amongst Judges of the courts. Be loud and clear in your arguments and never be disrespectful to the other side or to the court even if unpleasant words are hurled at you during the proceedings. Never get provoked. Be cool as a cucumber. The presentation skills are being watched by the court and judges will get an impression that you will never mislead, only if you behave in a level-headed manner. If you earn that reputation by putting in tireless efforts day in and day out, you will realise that subsequently you are being put to lesser scrutiny by the learned Judges whenever you argue a point. Convincing the court would then become easier. Also keep in mind that the client on the other side is also watching you closely when you make your representation. Be firm and stay with your side just like the adhesive on the stamps stick to one side until the envelope reaches its destination.

Sometimes you are liked by your opponents for your presentation skills and commitment. Towards the end of 2019, I had the occasion to represent one amongst two litigating brothers of a deceptively similar trade mark. One was a registered trade mark and the other claimed to be a prior user to the registered one. Both were owned by two blood brothers, who for various personal reasons had a strained relationship for quite some time. The case was aggressively argued and at one point the Judge instructed the parties to go for mediation and report settlement, since they were brothers. I must appreciate the kind cooperation of my client and also the advocates who appeared for the opposite party. Finally after repeated sessions of failed mediation, the matter was called in the chambers of the Hon'ble Judge and the ice broke. The case was settled in mediation in the chambers of the Learned Judge of the High court. The trade mark of our client that was unregistered was modified with some alteration to look different from his brother's registered trade mark and the same was accepted and the consent decree was passed. I was later approached by the opposite party , being impressed the way his elder brother's case was handled by me, to handle a personal case of his family member at Erode, which I gladly accepted as there was no contesting litigation in which I was appearing against him and since there was absolutely no clash of interest. Even then I informed my erstwhile client about the developments and he was surprised that I communicated this development to him and agreed with me to proceed without any further reference of the matter to him. Earn goodwill even amongst your opponent, it pays you for sure.

Honesty: Honesty is becoming a rare virtue these days. So if you practice it with a little extra effort, you will straightaway enter into the special and limited list of distinguished personalities. Be honest in your estimates in business and projections of the outcomes in the work that you promise to do for your clients, even if it is a little sour or bitter in the beginning. Your clients will realise and appreciate you for your honesty when the final result is closer to your prediction or if it comes out extremely good in their favour due to your dedicated approach. Be honest to the core.

I have detailed some of the self-management tools that can help you to become an accomplished lawyer and project you as an efficient professional to anyone, be it your client, the opponent's lawyer, the opposite party, the Learned Judge or even people who come for their cases in such courts where you make representations or arguments. Carry yourself well and with dignity. Don't let your personal bad habits (if any) be visible in courts and in public. Bad reputation spreads faster than Goodwill.

Inspiration

"There are no limits to what you can accomplish, except the limits you place on your own thinking."

-Brian Tracy, *Canadian-American motivational public speaker and self-development author*

Get inspired and stay inspired. To become a good lawyer, 'inspiration' is a major factor. Identify the best in the business in your chosen area of law. Observe their strengths and weaknesses. Try emulating their strengths in the possible manner and try to imbibe the skills to make them your strengths too. See how your icons have performed in the past. Nowadays it is very easy. Everything done by a Lawyer in court is getting electronically recorded in the website or the electronic case data collection and is being published. Don't be carried away by the exciting stories you hear about the iconic figure that inspires you. Have a scientific approach and support your decision to get inspired by an icon Lawyer, with sound statistics and evidence. Yes collection of evidence is very relevant in the profession of an advocate. Become an advocate for the icon you chose. Argue with yourself as to why you have chosen him or her as your professional inspiration. In the olden days in our Indian Culture, there was the concept of *'Maanasa Guru"* or 'Internal Master". You can adopt an Inspirational teacher without actually being his disciple. Watch them and learn from a distance even without his knowledge by accepting him in your mind as your master. Knowledge is knowledge, no matter from where it comes.

The next thing is that you need not confine yourself to just one 'internal master', you can have many. But ensure you have observed, acquired knowledge as much as possible, practiced sufficiently and achieved good results by applying what you have learnt before moving on to your next 'internal master' who has established his supremacy and authority in a totally different field of law. Subjects and field of practice are numerous and this exercise can be repeated any number of times during your life time. When you start doing this successfully your results too get uploaded in the form of reported judgments. You also become an icon for several young and aspiring lawyers, perhaps unknowingly. Get inspired and work hard to become an inspiration for the future generation to follow.

Luckily for me, I was fortunate enough to reach the office of one of the greatest Trial Lawyers of Karnataka on the criminal law practice, during my initial days where I was tested in fire. Truly, mine was not a baptism with water in the hands of Shri Tomy Sebastian but was indeed a baptism with fire! I was tutored, dictated upon, tested, checked on from time to time, sharpened my writing and oratory skills, etc., before graduating from what I would call the 'TS National Institute of Excellence in Trial Procedures'. Given an opportunity, I would love to be part of such a venture, if time and finances permit, for the benefit of upcoming lawyers who intend to practice litigation of all types. My all time and biggest inspiration has been Shri. Tomy Sebastian – Senior Advocate, Bangalore, so far as the practice of law as profession of advocacy is concerned. This breed of practitioners of law are on the decline and it is already very rare to find such a conservative Senior with a few Juniors who attach to him to gain knowledge that the Senior has acquired – almost like a Gurukul.

In sharp contrast, I see the glitz and glamour on the enrolment day near the BAR COUNCIL premises, from where some young lawyers start their independent practice without acquiring any skill or expertise in any branch of law. They learn at the cost of the clients by trial and error method. I strongly deprecate this practice. I myself practiced under the watchful eyes of a reputed Senior for almost five years before moving on to the most reputed Law Firm of South India and then staying there for almost a decade before deciding to commence my own law firm – Chennai Law Associates as detailed in the preceding chapters.

As I have stated earlier, on 9th February 2001 I commenced my Second Innings at the International Law firm in Chennai, where I was truly inspired to see the most humble lawyer of all times in the great Shri. P.S. SuranaJi. I have often reckoned that for his remarkable achievements on record the needn't be so humble. The practice followed by Surana Ji to greet each employee of the firm with folded hands when he entered the office was truly mesmerising to me. I was taught advanced courses in assessment of work, scope of work, rough time estimate of the job on hand, professional communication skills, case reporting to the management of the firm and client, maintenance of case records, invoicing professional fees and expenses, preparing for appellate procedures in case of setback at the trial court, resource management of both men and material and the strict compliance of all internal procedures as a part of the quality conscious deliverable to the client etc. He will forever continue to be a towering personality in my life – inspirational on the management front of my practice. I was spoon-fed the principles of trial by the great Senior Advocate Shri. Tomy Sebastian, Bangalore and tutored with care regarding all the commercial and management aspects of running a law firm by one of the greatest personalities in the legal industry Shri. P.S.Surana (Founder of Surana and Surana International Attorneys) before starting my own Law Firm.

While in Bangalore I was truly inspired with the judicial activism being taken upon by the Ramon Magsaysay Award winner Hon'ble Justice M.F.Saldhana who was involved in a lot of Public Interest Litigations back then in 1996-1999. Remarkable orders were passed by the inspiring Judges of the Karnataka High Court regarding the preservation of Cubbon Park from being converted into concrete jungles to house various government buildings, which was being considered by the then Karnataka Government. Yet another issue was about the stray dog menace in the CubbonPark. To stop the reproduction of stray dogs and allowing them to have a natural death, some outstanding orders were passed by the learned Judge. But these orders were always received with a pinch of salt as these orders were mostly passed after converting a letter addressed to the Judge or upon a Suo motto case being taken up upon seeing a News publishing. Later in March 2000, a bench of 5 Judges sat at the Karnataka High court which included some great names of Judges who went on to become outstanding Judges of the Hon'ble Supreme Court and quashed all the controversial Judgments of the Learned Judge M.F.Saldhana as they were said to be passed without jurisdiction. The courage to pass orders for the noble cause of protecting the environment inspired me a lot during my younger Bangalore days. His Lordship Mr. Justice R.V. Raveendran of the High Court of Karnataka, as he then was, was yet another Judge who inspired me, while I was in Bangalore. After I became active in my practice at Chennai, in October 2005 or so , I heard the happy news of the elevation of Justice R.V. Raveendran as a Judge of the Hon'ble Supreme Court. The joy I experienced was more due to the fact that he was one of my 'Internal Masters'. Thereafter, I followed some of the outstanding Judgments given by the learned Judge from the Apex Court that quenched my intellectual thirst and justified the faith I had in him as one my internal masters. The case laws on pendente-lite interests that gave a higher rate of interest for the plaintiffs during the pendency of the suit are still an authority on the subject.

In April 2006, I was a practising lawyer at the Madras High Court and I had a case before the Division bench of the Madras High Court, comprising the Bench of Justices R. Balasubramanian and Chitra Venkatraman JJ, wherein my opposing counsel was none other than Adv. V. Ramasubramanian, as he then was. The matter was a Civil Miscellaneous Appeal arising out of a Judgment of Divorce and the matter ended in a

Compromise. Yes it was none other than the distinguished Lordship Hon'ble Mr. Justice V. Ramasubramanian, present Supreme Court Judge, before being the Judge of Madras High Court, Andhra Pradesh High Court and The Chief Justice of Himachal Pradesh High Court. I appeared before him several times when he was in the Madras High court as a Judge. The ease with which he passed orders would demonstrate that the law did not permit any other order being passed and such that the lawyers who were at the losing end of the case also accept his orders gracefully. I had accepted him as yet another 'internal master' and followed his judgments all through and felt very inspired upon reading them, which reiterated the justification of the great man as one of my internal masters. The happiness with which I followed the stage-wise elevation of the learned Judge upto the Apex Court of India is limitless.

Some of the distinguished personalities in Chennai who have taken to my list of "Internal masters" are as under:

Hon'bleMr. JusticeManikumar – Chief Justice, Kerala High Court

Hon'ble Mr. Justice M. Satyanarayanan – Judge, High Court of Madras

Hon'ble Mr. Justice M. M.Sundaresh – Judge, High Court of Madras

Hon'ble Mr. Justice N. Kirubakaran – Judge, High Court of Madras

Hon'ble Mr. Justice M.S. Ramesh – Judge, High Court of Madras

Hon'ble Mr. Justice G.R. Swaminathan – Judge, High Court of Madras

Hon'ble Mr. Justice C.V. Karthikeyan – Judge, High Court of Madras

Hon'ble Mr. Justice N. Anand Venkatesh – Judge, High Court of Madras

Senior Advocate Shri. R.Krishnamoorthy

Senior Advocate Shri. N.R. Chandran

Senior Advocate Shri. V.T. Gopalan

Senior Advocate Shri. G. Masilamani

Senior Advocate Shri. Arvind Dattar

Senior Advocate Shri. Vijay Narayanan

Senior Advocate Shri. Ar.L. Sundaresan

Senior Advocate Shri. Aravindh Pandian

I recommend that the young readers who intend to make Litigation as a career after their enrolment to the respective bar councils, anywhere in the country, to make such a list and follow their work electronically from the available sources and also know more about them by observing them when in action during court hearings and learn as much as you can from these stalwarts whenever time permits. Along your way, you can keep adding to your list of *Internal Masters* as and when you stumble upon such personalities. Books can't give you all the learning that it takes to become a good advocate. Advocacy is an art; a complex art which involves several elements such as reading, writing, talking, maintaining silence in crucial times, acting to suit a particular role, a little bit of theatrics (not overacting and spoiling the show) and so on. A life time would be insufficient to master these arts by reading books and implementing them. So learn from all and be a vital learning resource to others. Get inspired. Be an inspiration for the young and bright future generation of lawyers.

Changing Times

"Intelligence is the ability to adapt to change."

-Stephen Hawking, *English theoretical physicist, cosmologist and author*

Over the past 3 decades, the legal profession has undergone dramatic changes and continues to do so Gone are the times when junior advocates would come with recommendations from Judges and people in High offices to get attached to a Senior advocate's office. The concept of an advocate's office being synonymous to Gurukuls also does not exist anymore. 'Learning without earning' has also become a practice of the past and every advocate office has started paying decently for fresh junior advocates so as to help sustain their livelihood according to the lifestyle in the respective cities of practice. The role of a stenographer has also become rare these days owing to the paid juniors who are more than willing to participate in the drafting process along-with the senior in their office, for the simple fact that these juniors very well understand that drafting is an important process of legal learning. Yet another drastic change from the practise of law thirty years ago to that of the modern days is that the legal research has become faster and more accurate with the advent of electronic libraries and websites providing case banks, e-journals, etc. A lawyer's office only has book shelves, volumes digests and journals for aesthetic appeal and luxurious ambience nowadays and all the material that we want to lay hands on is very much available on the internet without any dearth.

With the advent of the above changes, it has become hard to find a long standing junior advocate in any reputed advocate's office nowadays unless and until the juniors are related closely to the most important Senior in practise in that Law Firm or closely connected to the stakeholders of the firm. Under these circumstances, the rate of attrition or movement of migratory lawyers from one office to another is very high. The law firm culture is also one reason for the drastic change in the landscape of legal practice across the country. Campus interviews and fresh graduates in law are being taken into law firms for a package of CTC (Costs to the Company) by reputed Law firms across the country in their anxiety to harvest talents from campuses directly. This is also a reason for the changes on the ground so far as the practise of law as a profession is concerned. Access of internet to youngsters can also distract some of them too early and sometimes, even before completing 1 year in a lawyer's office or Law Firm, some such beginners start looking for greener pastures and more earnings. They compromise on proper learning and the young professionals keep hopping from one firm to another and end up being dissatisfied with every office they have been employed in and do not take home any great learning in their profession. The quest to strike gold instantly makes them become too ambitious too soon and they jump from one firm to the other too often. It is those juniors who practise the virtues of sacrifice and patience who strike Gold over a period of time. I have always maintained that this profession is akin to 'Mining' where the deeper you dig into at the right place, the more likely you are to hit the treasure chest of Gold and Diamonds. Patience and perseverance are the keys.

The more you do the more you learn, should be the attitude in an advocate's office. Grumbling when work is given may not be the right attitude. Do it happily. There is no small work or big work in a lawyer's office. In the beginning, I was asked to do the filings at the senior's office and also do all sorts of clerical works in the registry. Though I felt it was too small a work for an advocate, I realised the importance of knowing the clerical works when I stepped into the reputed Law Firm at Chennai. I had an edge over my other colleagues who depended on clerks for status updates on clerical works that were being handled by them. Work as team and treat your peers and junior colleagues in a cordial manner. If your team members are on work outside office, ensure that they eat properly amidst their work and be responsible to get the cost reimbursed from the office or let them collect it in advance from the seniors who entrusted the work. Respect each other and own up to mistakes without blaming others in the team. Advocates' offices are nowadays mostly open throughout the day, on average from around 8.30AM to around 8.30PM, Monday to Friday and at least up to 3.00PM on Saturdays, unlike being closed during court hours and reopening after 5.30PM which was being practiced earlier. Spend your time in court judiciously and observe maximum from the learned judges and other counsels while you wait for your case to be called. See that you return to your well-equipped desk at your office and continue your tasks on hand and whenever possible, spend time with your seniors in office and don't hesitate to ask them doubts, if you really want to learn. Accompany your senior to court unless and until you are specifically allotted other work by the senior. Manage your other court work efficiently and reach the court where the senior is performing.

The work in the chamber or office of the senior normally enables you to participate in the drafting works and client discussions which are the richest sources of learning. Learn the art of cross examination from your senior when he is performing at a trial. Assist your senior with a rough questionnaire for cross examinations. Even if the senior doesn't require it, prepare a questionnaire after reading the relevant pleadings and documents and when the senior performs the cross examination, match these questions and see whether you are travelling on the right track and whether you have understood the case properly. All these opportunities are now available in most of the offices and law firms and it is your will and inclination to work that matters and nothing else.

The bonding of a Senior-Junior relationship has also become rare with the advent of modern Law firms and migration of lawyers from one office to another and this also leads to the mushrooming of the least experienced juniors who take the brave plunge, without any experience or knowledge of practice areas. Similarly, multi-disciplinary practices have also become the order of the day. I strongly recommend that this multiple area practice be implemented after sufficient experience in each field. For any youngster to become a good advocate, I suggest he goes through the grind of a trial advocate's office for a considerable period of time (at least 3 years) before stepping into appellate side of practice. I can safely say that after doing enough labour at the trial court on the criminal and civil side of practice and after conducting sufficient cases in the appellate courts at Bangalore, I moved to the Law firm and went on to appear in all types of cases. The two offices where I worked cumulatively for almost 15 years, enabled me to appear at all stages of the case right from before a Magistrate's Court, Sessions Court, High Court Single benches and Division Benches and I also participated along-with other Senior advocates in the Hon'ble Supreme Court of India as well as assisted in post-conviction proceedings in the Supreme Court of Michigan at Detroit, USA. Similarly I have also worked at the Assistant City civil court or the court of Sub-Judge to the Hon'ble Supreme court at various stages of Civil Litigation as well. Apart from these types of cases, I was fortunate to work on complicated writ petitions, company petitions and appeals on the respective jurisdiction not only in the Madras High Court but also in several other High Courts during my tenure of 25 years of practice thus far. I had put in my entire efforts in several contested matters in the rent control courts, family courts, railway tribunals, debt recovery tribunals and the respective appellate tribunals, trade mark registry and the Intellectual property appellate board in several cases throughout my learning years. It is only after I worked on numerous matters of complicated nature and involving high stakes over a long period of time that I chose to commence my own practice at Chennai Law Associates. I suggest that upcoming lawyers who intend to start their own practice should work in different fields of law for at least 6 years before opting to practice on their own. The success you will enjoy will be immense if you adopt such a scientific approach. Nothing can substitute hands-on-experience in legal practice. We are constrained to change with the changing times.

Learn more and earn less.

Learn more and earn more.

Earn more and keep learning

These are the 3 golden stages to succeed in a career of law. I have learnt in my career that progress on the financial front and accumulation of knowledge was phased over a over a period of a minimum of 5 years between each stage. Though I was destined to go through these stages and it was not planned by me, I do suggest this as a planned approach for any new Lawyer who intends to commence his legal practice in an utmost professional manner. Success cannot evade you for long if you adapt to changing times.

A New Venture

"Only those who risk going too far can possibly find out how far one can go."

-T.S. Elliot, *Poet, playwright, publisher and editor.*

While moving hectically with the activities of Chennai Law Associates, one night in August 2017, when I returned home I saw a general countrywide monthly magazine of Physiotherapists, with articles and news relating to their profession. From the onwards, I often pondered as to why we can't start a monthly general magazine for the benefit of young lawyers and students. Finally, I looked up the formalities of Title registration and other procedures to be followed in getting the registration process completed with the RNI Delhi, which is the Government authority to grant the registration. The applications were sent, title verification completed and the entire process of registration was completed to the extent of commencement of publication of the monthly in the month of July 2019 and the Magazine – Chennai Lexlight was a reality and yet another dream come true for me and all at Chennai Law Associates, by September 2019.

I must record the great team efforts exhibited by a team of students from various Law Colleges across the country, who were interning at Chennai Law Associates, in making it possible from concept to hard print magazine in such a short span of time.

The format of the Magazine was finalised after careful deliberation with lawyers, law students and academicians from various universities. We decided to have two editorial boards to freeze and edit the contents worthy of publishing and there came into existence a student editorial board comprising of law students from various reputed law schools, perhaps for the first time in India, and the main Editorial Board consisting of lawyers. Chennai Lexlight commenced its beautiful journey with a bunch of talented youngsters willing to go the extra mile with us out of sheer love for the subject sharing opportunity. A handful of corporate clients of Chennai Law Associates chipped in with priceless contribution to take care of the cost of publication for at least a year by giving advertisements in support of the cause and out of affection towards me. Oh! What an experience it is turning out to be! Just six months into publication, the Magazine is fast earning praises from Judges of the Hon'ble High Courts, corporates and common folkfrom every walk of life, for the content and neat presentation of diversefields of law in simple English easily understandable to one and all.

The name was identified by me. Chennai Lexlight means – A magazine coming out from Chennai (CHENNAI) to spread the light (LIGHT) of legal (LEX) awareness to one and all. The logo was prepared within hours with the Silhouette of the heritage structure of the Madras High to symbolically represent CHENNAI & LEX the light radiating around it in the silhouette to mean LIGHT. The tagline was also finalised very soon as 'READ ENHANCE EXCEL'. The immense contribution of young and fresh minds made the task look so simple. Yet the outcome was indeed extremely professional. The cover design and the structure of contents that were to be permanent were formed as a template and the very first issue was published in September 2019.

Chennai Lexlight is a Non profitable venture and is aimed at creating widespread awareness of legal knowledge in a slow and steady manner, firstly to all stakeholders in the Legal Industry, then to the literate class and then perhaps to the less literate people. To make this achievable, it is kept in mind from day 1 that simple English will be the mode of expressing views in the magazine. Having been able to form a team of enthusiastic young lawyers and interns who are ever willing to learn and contribute, it will be a cardinal sin according to me, if I don't lead them to achievement of their major goal of feeding their intellect and make them give-back to the society in whatever way they can. This was the thought that resulted in the birth of Chennai Lexlight after all. The e-magazines have also been available on the website www.chennailexlight.com for subscription at a nominal fee so that legal awareness can be spread to a much wider audience.

The magazine helps us to reach out to the intelligent young minds who are part of great universities of law, as teachers and students of law, legal officers in private and public enterprises, advocates, judges of all courts and also people from different walks of life. The tremendous amount of goodwill it generates to the minds that work beyond their professional working hours, is one to experience as time goes on. We have been able to connect with several lawyers who practice in various distinct fields of law as experts, thereby enabling us to have a pool of specialised talents. The readers can also approach the lawyers who get their articles published on Chennai Lexlight platform and avail the services of such lawyers who are specialists in their respective fields of law, as the magazine introduces lawyers outside the firm to its readers. Thus an absolutely new vertical that integrates itself so very beautifully to various streams has been brought into existence successfully and I am sure it will mutually benefit the Firm and the readers of the monthly magazine.

To identify a new area of practice in law and to integrate it to the existing structure of the Law Firm by deputing responsible and efficient Advocates in those areas of practice is indeed the specialised job expected of a FULL SERVICE LAW FIRM. To look for innovative ideas and think out of the box to come up with outstanding outcomes, was what we were able to do at Chennai Law Associates through Chennai Lexlight. Even though we are just 6 months old and still at the infancy stage, I am sure this will go a long way to bring laurels to the Firm and its partners.

Yet another important object that is being achieved through the monthly magazine is the constant update of law from various courts in varied fields of law. The job satisfaction each and every member of the law firm who volunteer to work for the monthly magazine is due to this thirst for learning. This leads to the establishment of intellectual and stable work force.

The reach of the magazine to all quarters of high offices connected to the legal industry has imposed vigil of the highest order and the proof reading work cannot be delegated to persons without sufficient legal knowledge. The publication has to be responsible, error free and preferably without any political affiliations. The opportunity is out there for young lawyers to acquire knowledge updates from the Hon'ble Apex Court from time to time in various branches of law. Even though young advocates normally work in a specified branch of law such as Civil, Criminal, Banking, High court cases such as Appeals, revisions and Writ Petitions of specific nature that is allotted to them in their offices, their intellectual connect with the magazine helps them with an overall growth. For example a lawyer who attends to criminal cases will not get the opportunity to be updated about the latest views from the Hon'ble Supreme Court in Civil cases on a vast range of subjects. This knowledge can help aspiring candidates to prepare and attempt Judicial appointments as and when they are called for by the appropriate authorities. Thus, associating with the works of the monthly magazine slowly and steadily improves the knowledge base of these young aspiring lawyers and will add immensely to shaping their career in Law, be it practice of law or entering the Judicial services or even those who intend to move the corporate ladder.

Since the practice of law is one of the most challenging professions that needs constant updates in very many subjects from time to time, it is recommended that young lawyers volunteer to work on writing articles with regard to newer practice areas and/or change of laws by way of amendment to earlier law, ushering in progressive reforms and establishing tribunals and new types of special courts and Judicial authorities as brought in by legislature periodically, etc. I am certain that such efforts will draw enormous benefits in the long run individually.

Getting out of the comfort zone and doing more work than that what is normally required for handling your routine cases, is what can make you more competent and special than thousands of co-professionals out there. Identify your core area of Practice and keep doing constant, consistent and competent work in your core area of practice as much as you can and increase your visibility. Continuously strive to enhance your knowledge and get updated constantly and venture into newer areas of practice as and when opportunity knocks your door. Stay connected with academically rich and intellectual professional in the business and work on publishing papers and articles on varied subject of law by doing apt research and accumulation of appropriate materials and desertion of the same so as to demonstrate the better level of understanding of laws and skills that you possess over your collateral resources in the same field. I am extremely delighted that we could establish Chennai Lexlight to fulfil this important object of enhancing individual skills and knowledge. So, READ ENHANCE EXCEL.

Dream big, while you are awake.

"The best dreams happen when you're awake."

-Joshua J. Marine

The Way Forward

"If you're not moving forward, you're falling back."

-Sam Waterson, *American Actor, Director and Producer*

25 years is not a short span of time, but it is also not one giant leap. It is made up of one day at a time, one case at a time, bad and good days with failures and successes alternating to mould us and yet keep us humble for when we are sculpted. Perhaps, if life is kind to me, I would write another book 25 years from now on my half century in this profession, but I cannot imagine what my perspectives would be at that time. Because each day, with every case, with every client, with every co-worker and most importantly with ourselves, we are tuning ourselves without even knowing how the final composition will turn out. Each note plays an important role in a final melody – the highs, the lows, the harmonies, the instrumentals, the vocals, the background music, etc. and in the end, it is each of these individual aspects being put together that renders the final song complete!

You are on that journey now and I urge you to take it just the way it is – one step at a time. I have come a long way and I still have a long way to go, but looking back I can see that back then, I never would have imagined that the little everyday things I was doing just by showing up and persevering would make me rise the way they did.

When I got the results of my XII Board exams, I was not too pleased. I went to my father with my head bowed down and told him that I have not fared any great overall score. He looked at my report card and the first thing he said to me was "Son, look at your English marks! You have done extremely well in English and you have managed to pass the rest quite decently. You should always try to improve on your weaknesses but when you play, play to your strengths. Why don't you pursue your college education in English Literature?" I was truly lost for words. My beloved father did not scold me for my low marks on other subjects as I feared. He understood my insecurity and worry about the future and reassured me to pursue English with interest and that the rest of my path will reveal itself eventually. I never would have imagined that after that I would go on to attempt more courses and fumble with employment until my first and great guru Sri Tomy Sebastian chanced the beautiful career of litigation on me; that I would learn immeasurably and master the art of criminal law practice over the next 5 years; that I would go on to flourish for a decade long era under the guidance of Shri P.S. Surana and gain such unimaginable exposure and experience of a wide spectrum of legal areas or that I would finally reach my life's purpose of opening my own law firm, Chennai Law Associates and watch it flourish so well. And there can be

no doubt, my knowledge, grasp and interest in the English language so fondly encouraged by my dear father played its role in each of my drafts over my counterparts. But that is how life works – you walk towards the finish line on a trail-less path guided mostly by your conscience and the advice of your well-wishers and the sequence can only be seen when you look back.

Identify your strengths and weaknesses. Work tirelessly to improve your areas of weaknesses but more so, to strive in your areas of strengths. Trust that there is a path for you which will only reveal itself as time passes and all you can do is to be sincere and do your best one day at a time. Be good to your mentor, be good to your legal brethren, be good to your clients, be good to the legal system, be good to the law, be good to your conscience and be good to all those who you can help even if they cannot help you back. We must never forget that ours is a service first and profession next, so while you should earn all life's comforts that you want, do not hesitate to take time to also help those who deserve justice even if they cannot afford it. It is not a free service that you would be doing. Even though you may not be able to deposit it in a Bank, it will bring more comfort to you than any luxury you can ever imagine.

They say experience is life's greatest teacher, so the more you want to learn, the more you should be ready to fearlessly experience. "Come what may, I can handle it", should be your attitude towards any challenge posed before you. Do not shy away from more responsibilities in your area of interest, longer hours working at it and improving each time you fumble in it. Each case brings numerous experiences – you can learn from watching your seniors initially and then proceed to trying to tackle the stages of the cases one by one and only seeking the intervention of your senior for major stages and eventually, take up the challenge and try your hand at all stages! This is your learning period and on the learning curve, the only way is up. Our legal system is so wonderful that there is always a remedy for anything that goes wrong. So be bold, discuss your ideas and strategies with your seniors and brainstorm with peers and finally carry it out in the courtroom and see what happens. This is how you gain experience.

As I have laid focus even earlier in this book, it is my humble belief that juniors should stay at one place for longer in order to truly gain meaningful experience. This is because when you stay under the guidance of one senior for longer time, they can evaluate your strengths and weaknesses and advice you better to propel you in this field. Litigation is more practical and the art of advocacy cannot be mastered from any book. Only hands on experience and able guidance can capacitate you. The more you shift in the name of slightly better salaries or to get over minor complaints in your workplace, it only works like a rolling stone which rolls for a long distance but gathers no moss (in this case, meaningful experience). However, this is not to say that you should mandatorily stay at your job merely for the sake of it, even if the work entrusted to you is to your dissatisfaction over a period of time even after attempting to resolve it. Nobody can guide you as well as your conscience and gut.

Mentoring is an inherent part of advocacy and your mentor can make all the difference in the way your career us groomed. As long as the work and progress are to your satisfaction, try to adjust with the other aspects for the sake of your proper chiselling. Never forget the goal with which you entered this noble profession. You should definitely try to pan out into various kinds of work but never lose focus on your main career, since this is the time you have to work at it, fall, take help, get back up and work at it again and again and again till you reach a level of confidence and comfort to handle any case.

Inspiration does not come with a pompous announcement. It is hiding in plain sight, almost anywhere you look. You have to find it. Only will power can keep you grinding despite the initial low pay, lack of immediate results being visible to others, commitments to family and friends, etc. and will power has to be fuelled with inspiration for it to keep you running. Your mentor is always a subject of inspiration since they have achieved so much coming from where you are now and watching them excel everyday should be a reminder to keep going. We often wait for long hours in court rooms as it is a part and parcel of the nature of our work. A lot of people consider this a waste of time, but it is not necessarily so. While you wait in Court, try to go through your case bundle and know it inside out and try to think of the different angles to your case. Observe major arguments that take place in the Court on that day while you wait and jot down potential questions you may have on the legal aspect of such cases for you to research later. Observe the mannerisms of those who are arguing and the Judge's responses, for the art of advocacy is painted on the canvas of method of presentation – the law is the various shades of paint that have to be understood and experimented with to bring life to the paper, the concept of the art is the strategy you formulate from what you learnt out of experience and the portrayal of your concept is the presentation of your case on paper as well as finally in open Court before the Learned Judge. Your painting is incomplete without these ingredients.

I have seen many ups and downs over the last 2 and a half decades but the strife through it all has brought me where I am. Litigation is a beautiful profession and keeps us on our toes and promises not to let our days ever be dull. I wish every junior lawyer, law student and aspiring litigator the very best in all your endeavours and I am sure the profession will take you on a thrilling ride and perhaps one day, you would pay tribute to it, like I am doing today. These 25 years have turned out to be very kind to me when I look back now and I cannot wait to see what is in store for me for the rest of my ride. It is with utmost humility, eagerness and excitement that I continue on this beautiful journey and take my next step into my way forward!